Using Language Well
Book Three

English, Grammar, and Writing Points
from *Spelling Wisdom, Book Three*

Student Book

by Sonya Shafer

Using Language Well, Book Three, Student Book: English, Grammar, and Writing Points from *Spelling Wisdom, Book Three*
© 2018, 2021 by Sonya Shafer

Cover Design: John Shafer

ISBN 978-1-61634-429-0 printed
ISBN 978-1-61634-430-6 electronic download

Published by
Simply Charlotte Mason, LLC
930 New Hope Road #11-892
Lawrenceville, Georgia 30045
simplycharlottemason.com

Printed by PrintLogic, Inc.
Monroe, Georgia, USA

Contents

denotes the first time a topic is mentioned

* denotes the first time a topic is mentioned

denotes the first time a topic is mentioned

* denotes the first time a topic is mentioned

* denotes the first time a topic is mentioned

* denotes the first time a topic is mentioned

denotes the first time a topic is mentioned

How to Use This Book

Using Language Well, Book Three, is designed to be used alongside *Spelling Wisdom, Book Three.* You will need both books.

Spelling Wisdom books and *Using Language Well* teacher books are non-consumable and can be reused. *Using Language Well* student books are consumable; you will need one per student and a notebook for dictation exercises.

We recommend doing two lessons per week. At that pace this book will last two years: Lessons 1–70 in the first year, Lessons 71–140 in the second.

Most lessons take ten minutes or less to complete, plus the time spent to prepare for dictation.

Using Language Well, Book Three, assumes that you already know these parts of speech

- common noun
- proper noun
- pronoun
- article
- adjective
- adverb
- action verb
- helping verb
- linking verb
- preposition
- interjection
- conjunction

and can parse the italicized words in the following sentence.

> *Each of us has in his possession an exceedingly good servant or a very bad master,* known as Habit.

If you are not familiar with parts of speech or parsing, start with *Using Language Well, Book Two.*

Lesson 1
(from Exercise 1, Little Hammers)

1. Read Exercise 1 in *Spelling Wisdom, Book 3.*

2. Identify the part of speech of each italicized word in the sentence from Exercise 1. Parse above the words, using the following abbreviations:

PRO = pronoun	N = common noun	PN = proper noun	AV = action verb
LV = linking verb	HV = helping verb	ADJ = adjective	ART = article
ADV = adverb	PP = preposition	CON = conjunction	INT = interjection

    The habits of the child are, as it were, so *many little hammers* beating out *by slow degrees the*

    character of the man.

3. Now let's begin to analyze that sentence. Analyzing means to look at the jobs that the words are doing within the sentence in order to communicate the ideas contained in it. The parts of speech give us some clues, but the different words—and even groups of words—can do many different jobs. In this book you will always parse above the words and analyze below them.

    We'll start by reviewing the jobs of subject and predicate. Underline the three prepositional phrases in the sentence you parsed above, then look at the remaining italicized words and identify the simple subject and simple predicate verb. Write S below the simple subject and P below the simple predicate verb. (You'll learn about the jobs of the rest of the words as you progress through the lessons in this book.)

     Analyzing Tip: *Remember that a sentence can be divided into two main parts: the complete* subject *(that of which we speak) and the complete* predicate *(what we say about it). The* simple subject *and* predicate *will usually be just the main noun or pronoun of the subject with its verb.*

4. Prepare Exercise 1 for dictation by following these steps.

    »   Step One: Read the passage and identify words you don't know how to spell yet.

    »   Step Two: Study those words. Look at them carefully until you can close your eyes and see them in your mind.

    »   Step Three: Look closely at punctuation and capital letters. (Copy the exercise, if that will help you.)

    »   Step Four: When you are sure you know how to spell every single word in the exercise and are familiar with the punctuation and capitalization, ask your teacher to dictate it to you while you write it in a notebook.

Lesson 2
(from Exercise 2, Not To Excite Suspicion)

1. Read Exercise 2 in *Spelling Wisdom, Book 3.*

2. Identify the part of speech of each italicized word in the sentence from Exercise 2. Parse above the words, using the following abbreviations:

   PRO = pronoun   N = common noun   PN = proper noun   AV = action verb
   LV = linking verb   HV = helping verb   ADJ = adjective   ART = article
   ADV = adverb   PP = preposition   CON = conjunction   INT = interjection

   Not to excite suspicion *by her look or manner was now an object* **worth attaining.**

3. Underline the prepositional phrase. In a prepositional phrase, the preposition usually teams up with a noun or pronoun. That word is doing the job of the *object of the preposition*. You can find the object by saying the preposition and then asking, "What?" The noun or pronoun that answers that question is the object of the preposition.

   Before you look for the object of the preposition in this exercise's sentence, look back at the three prepositional phrases that you underlined in Lesson 1. Write them below and circle the object of each.

   _____

   _____

   _____

4. Now look at the prepositional phrase in the sentence you parsed above. What do you notice about its object?

   _____

   You have seen a compound subject and a compound predicate in previous lessons (in *Using Language Well, Book 2*). The sentence above contains a compound object of the preposition. Watch for more compound parts of a sentence in future lessons.

5. Prepare Exercise 2 for dictation by following these steps.

   » Step One: Read the passage and identify words you don't know how to spell yet.

   » Step Two: Study those words. Look at them carefully until you can close your eyes and see them in your mind.

   » Step Three: Look closely at punctuation and capital letters. (Copy the exercise, if that will help you.)

   » Step Four: When you are sure you know how to spell every single word in the exercise and are familiar with the punctuation and capitalization, ask your teacher to dictate it to you while you write it in a notebook.

Lesson 3
(from Exercise 3, True Happiness)

1. Read Exercise 3 in *Spelling Wisdom, Book 3.*

2. Identify the part of speech of each italicized word in the sentence from Exercise 3. Parse above the words, using the following abbreviations:

   PRO = pronoun   N = common noun   PN = proper noun   AV = action verb
   LV = linking verb   HV = helping verb   ADJ = adjective   ART = article
   ADV = adverb   PP = preposition   CON = conjunction   INT = interjection

   Many *persons have a wrong idea* of what constitutes true happiness.

3. Identify the simple subject and simple predicate verb. Remember to do your analyzing below the words. Write S below the simple subject and P below the simple predicate verb.

4. You learned last time about the object of a preposition. Sentences can have objects too. The *direct object* usually receives the direct action of an action verb. An easy way to identify the direct object is to say the simple subject and predicate, then ask, "What?" The noun or pronoun that answers that question is usually the direct object. Try it with the sentence you are analyzing above and write DO below the direct object.

5. Prepare Exercise 3 for dictation by following these steps.

   » Step One: Read the passage and identify words you don't know how to spell yet.

   » Step Two: Study those words. Look at them carefully until you can close your eyes and see them in your mind.

   » Step Three: Look closely at punctuation and capital letters. (Copy the exercise, if that will help you.)

   » Step Four: When you are sure you know how to spell every single word in the exercise and are familiar with the punctuation and capitalization, ask your teacher to dictate it to you while you write it in a notebook.

Lesson 4
(from Exercise 4, The Face of a Man)

1. Read Exercise 4 in *Spelling Wisdom, Book 3.*

2. Identify the part of speech of each italicized word in the clause from Exercise 4. Parse above the words, using the following abbreviations:

   PRO = pronoun   N = common noun   PN = proper noun   AV = action verb
   LV = linking verb   HV = helping verb   ADJ = adjective   ART = article
   ADV = adverb   PP = preposition   CON = conjunction   INT = interjection

   I *admire machinery* as much as *any man*.

3. Analyze the sentence by identifying the simple subject, simple predicate verb, and direct object. Write S below the simple subject, P below the simple predicate verb, and DO below the direct object.

4. Prepare Exercise 4 for dictation by following these steps.

   » Step One: Read the passage and identify words you don't know how to spell yet.

   » Step Two: Study those words. Look at them carefully until you can close your eyes and see them in your mind.

   » Step Three: Look closely at punctuation and capital letters. (Copy the exercise, if that will help you.)

   » Step Four: When you are sure you know how to spell every single word in the exercise and are familiar with the punctuation and capitalization, ask your teacher to dictate it to you while you write it in a notebook.

Lesson 5
(from Exercise 5, Gone Fishing)

1. Read Exercise 5 in *Spelling Wisdom, Book 3.*

2. Identify the part of speech of each word in the clause from Exercise 5. Parse above the words, using the following abbreviations:

PRO = pronoun	N = common noun	PN = proper noun	AV = action verb
LV = linking verb	HV = helping verb	ADJ = adjective	ART = article
ADV = adverb	PP = preposition	CON = conjunction	INT = interjection

   he baited his hook and threw it into the lake

3. Now analyze the clause by identifying the simple subject, simple predicate verb, and direct object. Write S below the simple subject, P below the simple predicate verb, and DO below the direct object.

4. Did you find the compound predicate verb and their two direct objects? (See Lesson 3 for a review if you need one.) Be sure to mark both verbs and direct objects.

5. Underline the prepositional phrase and circle the object of the preposition in that phrase.

6. Study the exercise until you are prepared for dictation.

Lesson 6
(from Exercise 6, Dishonesty)

1. Read Exercise 6 in *Spelling Wisdom, Book 3.*

2. Parse the following sentence from the exercise. Use this key to parse above the words:

PRO = pronoun	N = common noun	PN = proper noun	AV = action verb
LV = linking verb	HV = helping verb	ADJ = adjective	ART = article
ADV = adverb	PP = preposition	CON = conjunction	INT = interjection

    Don't trust that conventional idea.

3. What two words have been combined to form the contraction *don't?*

    _____

    _____

    What part of speech is each of those words? Be sure to parse them both in the sentence above.

4. Now let's analyze the sentence by labeling its subject (S), predicate verb (P), and direct object (DO) below the words. Notice that the subject is understood but not written into the sentence. Write the understood subject into the sentence where it belongs and label it underneath (S).

     Analyzing Tip: When analyzing a sentence, it is helpful to look for the verb first (the simple predicate). Once you have found the verb, you can ask "Who (verb)?" or "What (verb)?" The answer to that question will help you find the subject.

5. Study the exercise until you are prepared for dictation.

Lesson 7

(from Exercise 7, Contagious Laughter)

1. Read Exercise 7 in *Spelling Wisdom, Book 3.*

2. Charles Dickens was a master at selecting just the right words to convey just the right meanings. In this exercise he wanted to contrast two states of human living that are at opposite ends of a spectrum: *disease* and *sorrow* contrasted with *laughter* and *good humor.*

   He used a medical term to characterize each pair. Write those terms below:

   _____ **in disease and sorrow**

   _____ **as laughter and good humor**

   What ideas do those terms convey about disease and sorrow and laughter and good humor?

   _____

   _____

3. Now look closer at the other words he used to describe that situation of opposites. Grab a dictionary and define each word below. Some of them will have more than one possible meaning. Determine which meaning is the best fit in the context of Charles Dickens' sentence. Think about the idea that he was trying to convey.

   • fair _____

   • even-handed _____

   • noble _____

   • adjustment _____

4. Now that you have examined individual segments of the sentence, put it back together in your own words, incorporating what you have discovered. What does the sentence in Exercise 7 mean?

   _____

   _____

   _____

   _____

5. Those three consecutive adjectives you defined modify the same word: *adjustment.* What punctuation is used to separate them in the exercise?

   _____

   Watch future exercises to see whether that guideline holds true.

6. Study the exercise until you are prepared for dictation.

Lesson 8

(from Exercise 8, Dreams)

1. Read Exercise 8 in *Spelling Wisdom, Book 3*.

2. Notice this statement that Charles Dickens made:

   Dreams are the bright creatures of poem and legend, . . .

   Is that statement true? Are dreams actually creatures? Dickens used a figure of speech, a *metaphor*, to get his point across as a word picture. A figure of speech is an indirect way of explaining something by comparing it to something else. In the next clause he explained what he was thinking, why dreams are like creatures. Read the rest of the exercise again and put his explanation in your own words.

   _____

   _____

   _____

3. Come up with your own metaphor about dreams. Write a sentence that states, "Dreams are _____" and explain the meaning of your metaphor.

   _____

   _____

   _____

   _____

4. Notice that a metaphor does not overtly say, "This is *like* that." It paints a word picture and says, "This *is* that." Look at the sentence in Exercise 1 for another metaphor. Charlotte Mason said that

   _____ are _____.

   In what way is that comparison true?

   _____

   _____

   _____

   ✎ ***Writing Point:*** *Good metaphors can carry a lot of impact in your writing.*

5. Study the exercise until you are prepared for dictation. Notice that commas separate each of the three clauses in the sentence.

Lesson 9
(from Exercise 9, Ecclesiastes 12:13, 14)

1. Read Exercise 9 in *Spelling Wisdom, Book 3*.

2. Parse and analyze the following clause from the exercise. Use the key at the bottom of this page to help you. (Check Lesson 6, #4, if you need a reminder about how to mark an understood subject.)

    Fear God and keep his commandments

    Analyzing Tip: Remember to look for the verb first when analyzing a sentence (the simple predicate). Then ask "Who (verb)?" or "What (verb)?" to find the subject.

3. Tell all you know about a direct object.

    _____

    _____

    _____

    _____

    _____

4. Study the exercise until you are prepared for dictation.

Parse above the words:	PRO = pronoun	N = common noun	PN = proper noun	AV = action verb
	LV = linking verb	HV = helping verb	ADJ = adjective	ART = article
	ADV = adverb	PP = preposition	CON = conjunction	INT = interjection
Analyze below the words:	S = simple subject	P = simple predicate	DO = direct object	

Lesson 10
(from Exercise 10, They Are Both Men)

1. Read Exercise 10 in *Spelling Wisdom, Book 3*.

2. We have been using the terms *clause* and *phrase* throughout these lessons as you parse and analyze. Both clauses and phrases are groups of words, but there is a key difference between them. Take a look at some of the clauses and phrases you have seen in the lessons so far (listed below), compare them, and see what you notice about the difference between them.

Clauses
I admire machinery as much as any man
he baited his hook and threw it into the lake
Dreams are the bright creatures of poem and legend
Fear God and keep his commandments

Phrases
of the child
by slow degrees
of the man
by her look or manner

The main difference(s) you noticed:

_____

_____

_____

Hint: Think about what parts of speech and parts of a sentence you see in one column but not the other.

3. Now look at these groups of words from Exercise 10 and determine which are clauses and which are phrases. A clause will have both a verb and its subject. Write a *C* beside each clause and a *P* beside each phrase.

they are both men

men of different races and colors

with the same nature

Both have souls

both will be held accountable

for their deeds

in this life

4. Study the exercise until you are prepared for dictation.

Lesson 11
(from Exercise 11, A Swarm of Bees Worth Hiving)

1. Read Exercise 11 in *Spelling Wisdom, Book 3*.

2. In this lesson let's take a break from analyzing sentences and talk a bit about poetry. You will find several poem exercises sprinkled throughout this book, and each time you come upon one, you will learn a bit more about analyzing poetry. The easiest place to start analyzing poetry is with rhymes.

   A rhyme is a similar sound found in two different words, such as *mild* and *child*. If you find the rhyming words at the end of the lines of the poem, they are called *end rhymes*. List the end rhymes below that you find in the poem in Exercise 11.

   mild, child
   _____

   _____

   _____

   _____

   _____

   _____

   _____

3. You'll notice that end rhymes are not always spelled the same, but they should sound the same. Put a box around the end rhymes that sound similar but are spelled with different vowel combinations.

4. Now look at all of the end rhymes again. Which pair do you think gives the strongest end rhyme? Circle it. Which pair do you think gives the weakest end rhyme? Put a question mark beside it.

5. Who or what was Solon, mentioned in the second line of the poem? Check a dictionary or encyclopedia.

   _____

   _____

6. Study the poem until you are prepared for dictation.

Lesson 12
(from Exercise 12, A Great Charm)

1. Read Exercise 12 in *Spelling Wisdom, Book 3*.

2. Parse and analyze the following sentence from the exercise. Use the key at the bottom of this page to help you.

    Poverty certainly has not contracted her mind.

    Analyzing Tip: Once you have found the verb and its subject, look for the typical pattern often seen in sentences. If the verb is an action verb, look for this common pattern: Subject – Action Verb – Direct Object. Not all sentences will have a direct object, but many of them will.

3. What does *contracted* mean in the context of that sentence? Look up the word's possible definitions in a dictionary and determine which meaning fits best here.

    _____

    _____

4. How might poverty contract a person's mind?

    _____

    _____

    _____

    _____

5. Study the exercise until you are prepared for dictation.

Parse above the words:	PRO = pronoun	N = common noun	PN = proper noun	AV = action verb
	LV = linking verb	HV = helping verb	ADJ = adjective	ART = article
	ADV = adverb	PP = preposition	CON = conjunction	INT = interjection
Analyze below the words:	S = simple subject	P = simple predicate	DO = direct object	

Lesson 13
(from Exercise 13, Scrooge)

1. Read Exercise 13 in *Spelling Wisdom, Book 3*.

2. Parse and analyze the following sentence from the exercise. Use the key at the bottom of this page to help you.

   External heat and cold had little influence on Scrooge.

3. What is the coordinating conjunction *and* joining? _____

   So that sentence has a compound _____.

4. The clause that you analyzed in Lesson 9 has a compound _____.

5. Study the exercise until you are prepared for dictation.

Parse above the words:	PRO = pronoun	N = common noun	PN = proper noun	AV = action verb
	LV = linking verb	HV = helping verb	ADJ = adjective	ART = article
	ADV = adverb	PP = preposition	CON = conjunction	INT = interjection
Analyze below the words:	S = simple subject	P = simple predicate	DO = direct object	

Lesson 14

(from Exercise 14, Make Progress)

1. Read Exercise 14 in *Spelling Wisdom, Book 3*.

2. Parse and analyze the following sentence from the exercise. Use the key at the bottom of this page to help you.

   Every day you may make progress.

3. The next sentence in the exercise contains a *subject complement* rather than a direct object. You will remember that a direct object is a word in the predicate part of the sentence that receives the action of the verb. A subject complement also comes in the predicate part of the sentence, but it completes the subject by either naming it or describing it. (That's why it is called a subject complement.) If the subject complement *names* the subject, it is a *predicate nominative*; if it describes the subject, it is a *predicate adjective*.

   The tip off for a subject complement will be the verb. If it is an action verb, look for a direct object to receive that action. If it is a linking verb, it will be linking the subject to its complement.

   Look for the subject complement as you parse and analyze the following sentence from the exercise. Use the key at the bottom of this page to help you.

   Every step may be fruitful.

4. Parse and analyze the following clause from Exercise 12. You should find another subject complement in it. Use the key at the bottom of this page to help you.

   nobody is afraid of her

    Analyzing Tip: Now you know the three main patterns to look for when analyzing sentences:
   - » *Sentence Pattern 1: Subject – Action Verb – Direct Object*
   - » *Sentence Pattern 2: Subject – Linking Verb – Predicate Nominative (noun)*
   - » *Sentence Pattern 3: Subject – Linking Verb – Predicate Adjective (adjective)*

5. Study Exercise 14 until you are prepared for dictation.

Parse above the words:	PRO = pronoun	N = common noun	PN = proper noun	AV = action verb
	LV = linking verb	HV = helping verb	ADJ = adjective	ART = article
	ADV = adverb	PP = preposition	CON = conjunction	INT = interjection
Analyze below the words:	S = simple subject	P = simple predicate	DO = direct object	PN = predicate nominative
	PA = predicate adjective			

Lesson 15
(from Exercise 15, A Sprinkling of Powder)

1. Read Exercise 15 in *Spelling Wisdom, Book 3*.

2. Parse and analyze the following clause from the exercise. Use the key at the bottom of this page to help you.

   He wore a sprinkling of powder upon his head

3. Underline the two prepositional phrases within that clause and circle the object of each phrase.

4. Have you ever noticed that prepositional phrases act like modifiers? They give additional information to help you modify the mental picture that is forming in your head as you read the sentence. In that respect, they work as an adjective or an adverb does.

   Look closely at the clause you analyzed above and determine what word each prepositional phrase is modifying. If it modifies a noun or pronoun, it is doing the job of an adjective, so it is called an *adjective phrase*. If it modifies a verb or another adjective, it is doing the job of an *adverb phrase*. On the lines below, write each prepositional phrase, the word that it modifies, and the job it is doing (either adjective or adverb).

Phrase	Modifies	Job
_____	_____	_____
_____	_____	_____

5. Study the exercise until you are prepared for dictation.

Parse above the words:	PRO = pronoun	N = common noun	PN = proper noun	AV = action verb
	LV = linking verb	HV = helping verb	ADJ = adjective	ART = article
	ADV = adverb	PP = preposition	CON = conjunction	INT = interjection
Analyze below the words:	S = simple subject	P = simple predicate	DO = direct object	PN = predicate nominative
	PA = predicate adjective			

---

simplycharlottemason.com

Lesson 16
(from Exercise 16, The Society of Authors)

1. Read Exercise 16 in *Spelling Wisdom, Book 3*.

2. For each prepositional phrase given below, tell what word in the exercise it modifies and what job the phrase is doing: adjective or adverb.

Phrase	Modifies	Job
to us	_____	_____
of people	_____	_____
of the very first rank	_____	_____

3. This exercise contains a metaphor. Tell what a metaphor is. (Look back at Lesson 8 for a reminder if you need it.)

   _____

   _____

4. What metaphor is in this exercise? Explain the word picture, the comparison, in your own words.

   _____

   _____

   _____

   _____

5. Study the exercise until you are prepared for dictation.

Lesson 17
(from Exercise 17, Sailing Over Angry Waters)

1. Read Exercise 17 in *Spelling Wisdom, Book 3*.

2. For each prepositional phrase given below, tell what word in the exercise it modifies and what job the phrase is doing: adjective or adverb.

Phrase	Modifies	Job
over a boundless expanse		
of sea		
on every side		
in the howling storm		
in ribbons		
from the mast		

3. The word *boundless* contains a suffix that changes the root word's meaning and part of speech.

   What is the root word of *boundless?* _____

4. Look up that root word in a dictionary. Note what part of speech it is in the sentence in the exercise and find the corresponding definition for that part of speech in the dictionary.

   _____

5. Explain how the suffix *-less* changes the word's definition.

   _____

   _____

   _____

6. Study the exercise until you are prepared for dictation.

Lesson 18
(from Exercise 18, The Best Actor)

1. Read Exercise 18 in *Spelling Wisdom, Book 3*.

2. Parse and analyze the following clause from the exercise. Use the key at the bottom of this page to help you.

   Mr. Crawford was considerably the best actor of all

 Analyzing Tip: *When looking for the predicate verb and its subject, it can be helpful to narrow down your options. You can disregard any modifiers in the sentence, whether they are single words or prepositional phrases. If they are doing the job of modifying, they won't be subjects or predicate verbs.*

3. Write down all that you know about clauses and phrases.

   _____

   _____

   _____

   _____

4. What do you know about subject complements?

   _____

   _____

   _____

   Writing Point: *Remember, the linking verb is a key for both the predicate nominative and the predicate adjective. Make sure you know the common linking verbs so you can use them all in your writing and not get stuck in a rut, reusing the same one(s) repeatedly. (See page 155 for a list.)*

5. Study the exercise until you are prepared for dictation.

Parse above the words:	PRO = pronoun	N = common noun	PN = proper noun	AV = action verb
	LV = linking verb	HV = helping verb	ADJ = adjective	ART = article
	ADV = adverb	PP = preposition	CON = conjunction	INT = interjection
Analyze below the words:	S = simple subject	P = simple predicate	DO = direct object	PN = predicate nominative
	PA = predicate adjective			

Lesson 19

(from Exercise 19, Grow in Christlikeness)

1. Read Exercise 19 in *Spelling Wisdom, Book 3*.

2. Write two synonyms for each of the following words from the exercise. Check a thesaurus for helpful suggestions.

recognition _____ _____

hesitates _____ _____

abandon _____ _____

extenuating _____ _____

confesses _____ _____

forsakes _____ _____

3. Now summarize in your own words the author's three points about a person who is apt to grow in Christlikeness.

_____

_____

_____

_____

_____

_____

_____

_____

Writing Point: *Notice how the author used the same pronoun-with-present-tense-verb construction for his three main points:* who lets, who (never) hesitates, who (promptly) confesses and forsakes. *Consistency like that (sometimes called* parallel construction*) helps the reader easily identify your points.*

4. Study the exercise until you are prepared for dictation.

Lesson 20

(from Exercise 20, Loyal Sympathy)

1. Read Exercise 20 in *Spelling Wisdom, Book 3*.

2. Determine whether each group of words below, taken from the exercise, is a clause or a phrase. Write *C* beside each clause and *P* beside each phrase. If it is a phrase, also give the word from the exercise that the phrase is modifying and identify whether it is doing the job of an adjective phrase or an adverb phrase.

   of affection and regard _____

   when all other eyes are turned coldly away _____

   of one being _____

   when all others have deserted us _____

   in the deepest affliction _____

   which no wealth could purchase _____

3. Notice how the author used dashes to set off the middle portion of the sentence. What does that part contribute to the sentence?

   _____

   _____

   Why do you suppose he set it off with punctuation that way?

   _____

   _____

   Watch for dashes in future exercises and see if they are used in the same way.

4. Study the exercise until you are prepared for dictation.

Lesson 21

(from Exercise 21, At the Abbey)

1. Read Exercise 21 in *Spelling Wisdom, Book 3*.

2. Find the phrase in the exercise that fits each description below and record the missing information.

Phrase	Modifies	Job
_____	*had been*	_____
of her father's comfort	_____	_____
_____	*understanding*	_____
to her and all her family	_____	_____

3. What does the portion set off with the dash add to the sentence?

   _____

   _____

4. So when should you use a dash in your writing? (Take a look at how a dash is used in Exercises 10, 12, and 16 to confirm your findings.)

   _____

   _____

5. Study the exercise until you are prepared for dictation.

Lesson 22

(from Exercise 22, My Little Book)

1. Read Exercise 22 in *Spelling Wisdom, Book 3*.

2. Now read the poem again slowly, clause by clause, and don't move on to the next clause until you can put the current one into your own words. How would you summarize in one sentence what John Bunyan said about his book, *The Pilgrim's Progress?*

   _____

   _____

3. Now that you know what the poem says, let's take a look at its end rhymes. (Check Lesson 11 if you need a reminder about end rhymes.) Write the end rhyme words below, one word per line.

   _____

   _____

   _____

   _____

   _____

   _____

   _____

   _____

   _____

   _____

4. One interesting part of analyzing a poem is discovering how the poet arranged the rhyming words. That arrangement is called a *rhyme scheme*. Look at the pairs of end rhymes you listed and assign a letter to each rhyme sound. Write an *A* beside the first sound: *dwell.* Now look at the next word you listed. Does it have the same sound or a different one? If it has the same sound, write an *A* beside it; if different, give it a different letter (*B*, for instance). Continue to work your way down the list of end rhymes and assign a different letter to each unique rhyme sound you discover *(A, B, C, D)*.

5. Now write your letters in a row to summarize that poem's rhyme scheme, or pattern.

   _____

6. Study the poem until you are prepared for dictation.

Lesson 23
(from Exercise 23, Jean Louis Ernest Meissonier)

1. Read Exercise 23 in *Spelling Wisdom, Book 3*.

2. Parse and analyze the following clause from the exercise.

    His work was called "microscopic"

 Analyzing Tip: *Remember to look for the three main patterns in a sentence:*
   » *Sentence Pattern 1: Subject – Action Verb – Direct Object*
   » *Sentence Pattern 2: Subject – Linking Verb – Predicate Nominative (noun)*
   » *Sentence Pattern 3: Subject – Linking Verb – Predicate Adjective (adjective)*

3. Explain the difference between a phrase and a clause.

    _____

    _____

4. Find one adjective prepositional phrase in the exercise. Write it below along with the word it modifies.

    _____

5. The two words below contain suffixes. For each, give its part of speech with the suffix, its root word, and its part of speech without the suffix.

Word	Part of Speech	Root Word	Part of Speech
exquisitely	_____	_____	_____
microscopic	_____	_____	_____

6. Study the exercise until you are prepared for dictation. Remember, commas and periods always go inside quotation marks.

Parse above the words:	PRO = pronoun	N = common noun	PN = proper noun	AV = action verb
	LV = linking verb	HV = helping verb	ADJ = adjective	ART = article
	ADV = adverb	PP = preposition	CON = conjunction	INT = interjection
Analyze below the words:	S = simple subject	P = simple predicate	DO = direct object	PN = predicate nominative
	PA = predicate adjective			

simplycharlottemason.com

Lesson 24
(from Exercise 24, A Mere Unit)

1. Read Exercise 24 in *Spelling Wisdom, Book 3.*

2. Near the end of the sentence you will find the words *importance* and *magnitude*. What job in the sentence are those two nouns performing together?

    _____

3. Since the two words are joined by the conjunction *and,* they are considered a compound object of a preposition. Look closely at the exercises listed below and find the compound object of a preposition that each one contains.

    • Exercise 8 _____

    • Exercise 14 _____

    • Exercise 20 _____

4. Check a dictionary to help you define the words below, keeping in mind the context of the sentence.

    • unit _____

    • dispossess _____

    • facility _____

    • magnitude _____

5. Summarize your findings by writing the sentence's idea in your own words.

    _____

    _____

    _____

    _____

6. Some people get *lose* confused with *loose*. While you have your dictionary handy, look up the meaning of each of those words to help you use the correct one in the sentence.

    • Lose _____

    • Loose _____

7. Study the exercise until you are prepared for dictation.

Lesson 25
(from Exercise 25, The Letter)

1. Read Exercise 25 in *Spelling Wisdom, Book 3*.

2. Look through Exercises 1–25 and make note of the book titles from which those exercises were taken. Alphabetize those titles below, omitting duplicates. (Tip: Disregard the articles *a, an,* and *the* when at the beginning of a title. Move articles to the end of the listing, preceded by a comma; for example, *Adventures of Sherlock Holmes, The.*)

_____

_____

_____

_____

_____

_____

_____

_____

_____

_____

_____

3. Study the exercise until you are prepared for dictation.

Lesson 26
(from Exercise 26, Storms of Adversity)

1. Read Exercise 26 in *Spelling Wisdom, Book 3*.

2. Parse and analyze the following sentence from the exercise. It's a long sentence, so take your time and be on the lookout for a compound predicate verb and several direct objects.

   The storms of adversity, like the storms of the ocean, rouse the faculties and excite the invention,

   prudence, skill, and fortitude of the voyager.

   Analyzing Tip: When looking for the predicate verb and its subject, narrow down your options by disregarding any modifiers.

3. The phrase "like the storms of the ocean" conveys another figure of speech. What is meant by *figure of speech*? (See Lesson 8 for a reminder.)

   _____

   _____

4. This figure of speech is called a *simile* (SIM-ih-lee). A simile is more obvious than a metaphor, because it comes right out and says this is *like* that or *as* that. How would you rewrite the sentence above using a metaphor instead of the simile?

   _____

   _____

   _____

   _____

5. Study the exercise until you are prepared for dictation.

Parse above the words:	PRO = pronoun	N = common noun	PN = proper noun	AV = action verb
	LV = linking verb	HV = helping verb	ADJ = adjective	ART = article
	ADV = adverb	PP = preposition	CON = conjunction	INT = interjection
Analyze below the words:	S = simple subject	P = simple predicate	DO = direct object	PN = predicate nominative
	PA = predicate adjective			

Lesson 27
(from Exercise 27, Injustice)

1. Read Exercise 27 in *Spelling Wisdom, Book 3*.

2. What does the phrase "as many hands high" mean in this context? Do some Internet research (with adult supervision) to find out the connection between that phrase and a horse.

   _____

   _____

3. Now put into your own words the idea that Charles Dickens was trying to communicate. What do those two sentences mean?

   _____

   _____

   _____

   _____

   _____

4. Why are there dashes in the first sentence of the exercise?

   _____

   _____

5. Study the exercise until you are prepared for dictation.

Lesson 28

(from Exercise 28, Threatened with My Presence)

1. Read Exercise 28 in *Spelling Wisdom, Book 3.*

2. Parse and analyze the following clause from the exercise.

you are threatened with my presence from the 18th to the 22nd of next December

⌕ *Analyzing Tip: This sentence will be much easier to analyze once you disregard all the modifiers.*

3. Define each word listed below; then, without looking at the exercise, determine which homonym from each set belongs in the given statements.

- no _____

- know _____

- knot _____

- not _____

   I _____ .

- presence _____

- presents _____

   You are threatened with my _____.

- dear _____

- deer _____

- to _____

- two _____ _____

- too _____

   Your friendship is _____ _____ me.

4. Study the exercise until you are prepared for dictation.

Parse above the words:	PRO = pronoun	N = common noun	PN = proper noun	AV = action verb
	LV = linking verb	HV = helping verb	ADJ = adjective	ART = article
	ADV = adverb	PP = preposition	CON = conjunction	INT = interjection
Analyze below the words:	S = simple subject	P = simple predicate	DO = direct object	PN = predicate nominative
	PA = predicate adjective			

Lesson 29

(from Exercise 29, Towards the House)

1. Read Exercise 29 in *Spelling Wisdom, Book 3*.

2. Parse and analyze the following clause from the exercise.

   withered leaves crackled and snapped beneath his feet

3. Find the simile in the first sentence of the exercise. Record it below and explain what is being compared. (Look up the definition of any unfamiliar words.)

   _____

   _____

4. What do you know about the difference between a simile and a metaphor?

   _____

   _____

   _____

5. Three words in the exercise have an *-ly* suffix. Detail each one's part of speech with the suffix, root word, and part of speech without the suffix.

Word	Part of Speech	Root Word	Part of Speech
softly	_____	_____	_____
cheerily	_____	_____	_____
sweetly	_____	_____	_____

6. Study the exercise until you are prepared for dictation.

Parse above the words:	PRO = pronoun	N = common noun	PN = proper noun	AV = action verb
	LV = linking verb	HV = helping verb	ADJ = adjective	ART = article
	ADV = adverb	PP = preposition	CON = conjunction	INT = interjection
Analyze below the words:	S = simple subject	P = simple predicate	DO = direct object	PN = predicate nominative
	PA = predicate adjective			

Lesson 30
(from Exercise 30, The Man of Business)

1. Read Exercise 30 in *Spelling Wisdom, Book 3*.

2. Find the two three-term series given in the exercise. List each series below.

   _____   _____

   _____   _____

   _____   _____

3. The first series are consecutive adjectives that all modify what word in the sentence?

   _____

   Does the punctuation guideline that you noticed in Exercise 7 hold true?

4. Which guideline on page 153 applies to the second three-term series in the sentence?

   _____

   _____

5. Define *latter*. Use a dictionary if you need help.

   _____

   _____

   To which word in the exercise does *latter* refer? _____

6. What are *gaiters*?

   _____

   _____

7. Study the exercise until you are prepared for dictation.

Lesson 31
(from Exercise 31, Sunshine)

1. Read Exercise 31 in *Spelling Wisdom, Book 3*.

2. Read the first sentence of the exercise again. What synonym could you use in place of *yet*, considering the context?

   _____

3. Read the last sentence of the exercise. The sun's glare served to bring forward stains and dirt in the parlor. How did Jane Austen describe those stains and dirt?

   _____

4. Now, we both know that stains and dirt do not actually sleep. The author attributed to an object something that humans do. You have just discovered another figure of speech: *personification*. How would you define *personification* in your own words?

   _____

   _____

5. Look back at Exercise 29 and find another personification.

   _____

   _____

6. Study the exercise until you are prepared for dictation.

Lesson 32

(from Exercise 32, How Do I Love Thee?)

1. Read Exercise 32 in *Spelling Wisdom, Book 3.*

2. Let's take a break from grammar and think about this poem. What is the tone of this poem? Imagine that the poet is speaking those words aloud. Would her voice convey sorrow? glee? boredom? patriotism? Think about the emotion behind the words and describe the tone of the poem.

   _____

3. What words in the poem do you think contribute to that tone?

   _____

4. See if you can figure out this poem's rhyme scheme. The end-rhyme words are already listed for you below. Assign a letter to each rhyme sound you find.

   _____ ways

   _____ height

   _____ sight

   _____ Grace

   _____ day's

   _____ light

   _____ Right

   _____ Praise

   _____ use

   _____ faith

   _____ lose

   _____ breath

   _____ choose

   _____ death

   Writing Point: End rhymes do not always need to come at the ends of sentences. Don't automatically pause at the end of each line. Read the poem according to the punctuation marks, as you would any other sentence, to best understand the poet's meaning. Keep that idea in mind when you write your own poems.

5. Do you see any patterns? Try dividing the scheme into four sections: four lines, four lines, three lines, three lines. Congratulations, you have just discovered a common rhyme scheme for a sonnet. Write the rhyme scheme below and count the number of lines.

   _____

   A sonnet is a poem of fourteen lines that follows a strict rhyme scheme and structure. The exact scheme has been tweaked over the centuries according to particular poets' tastes, but it will always have fourteen lines and a recognizable structure similar to the one you marked above.

6. Study the poem until you are prepared for dictation.

Lesson 33
(from Exercise 33, Writing a Letter)

1. Read Exercise 33 in *Spelling Wisdom, Book 3*.

2. Parse and analyze the following sentence from the exercise. Hint: The word *although* is considered both an adverb and a conjunction.

   These motions, although unquestionably of the greatest assistance to original composition,

   retard in some degree the progress of the writer.

3. Notice the phrases between the subject and the predicate verb. Why do you suppose they are there? Try reading the sentence without them. Does their omission change the sentence's meaning? It's almost as if those phrases are an aside. The sentence could be written with parentheses around those phrases and still be understood. That's why phrases like that are often referred to as *parenthetical phrases*—just a little extra information brought in on the side. What do you notice about how they are set off by punctuation?

   _____

   Watch for other parenthetical phrases in future exercises and see if they feature the same punctuation.

    Writing Point: *Parenthetical phrases can make writing sound more conversational. People often insert asides as they talk; a parenthetical phrase does the same job in writing. Moderation, of course, is key. Too many can make your composition choppy and hard to read, but one or two, inserted well, can help convey your personality and writing voice.*

4. You will recall that phrases can do the job of modifiers. For each prepositional phrase given below, tell what word in the exercise it modifies and what job the phrase is doing: adjective or adverb.

Phrase	Modifies	Job
of the greatest assistance	_____	_____
to original composition	_____	_____
in some degree	_____	_____
of the writer	_____	_____

5. Study the exercise until you are prepared for dictation.

Parse above the words:	PRO = pronoun	N = common noun	PN = proper noun	AV = action verb
	LV = linking verb	HV = helping verb	ADJ = adjective	ART = article
	ADV = adverb	PP = preposition	CON = conjunction	INT = interjection
Analyze below the words:	S = simple subject	P = simple predicate	DO = direct object	PN = predicate nominative
	PA = predicate adjective			

Lesson 34
(from Exercise 34, Midnight)

1. Read Exercise 34 in *Spelling Wisdom, Book 3.*

2. What does the word *but* mean in the following sentence from the exercise? Consider the context.

_____

The wind, high and boisterous but now, has died away and hoarsely mutters in its sleep.

3. Now parse and analyze that sentence, keeping in mind what *but* means in it.

   Analyzing Tip: Remember to disregard all the modifiers when looking for the predicate verb and its subject.

4. Do you see a parenthetical phrase in that sentence? What is it?

_____

   What job is it doing in the sentence?

_____

   What punctuation is used to set it off? How does that compare to the parenthetical phrases in Lesson 33?

_____

_____

5. The sentence from the exercise also contains a personification figure of speech. (See Lesson 31 for a reminder.) Tell what *personification* is and explain where you find it in the sentence above.

_____

_____

_____

_____

6. Study the exercise until you are prepared for dictation.

Parse above the words:	PRO = pronoun	N = common noun	PN = proper noun	AV = action verb
	LV = linking verb	HV = helping verb	ADJ = adjective	ART = article
	ADV = adverb	PP = preposition	CON = conjunction	INT = interjection
Analyze below the words:	S = simple subject	P = simple predicate	DO = direct object	PN = predicate nominative
	PA = predicate adjective			

Lesson 35

(from Exercise 35, Holding My Breath)

1. Read Exercise 35 in *Spelling Wisdom, Book 3.*

2. Find a parenthetical phrase in the following clause from the exercise and underline it. (Remember, a phrase does not have a verb and its subject.)

I was ready to burst with holding my breath, when, as I felt myself rising up, so, to my immediate

relief, I found my head and hands shoot out above the surface of the water

3. What punctuation sets that parenthetical phrase off in the sentence?

_____

4. Look back at the first sentence of the exercise. What job is the dash doing?

_____

_____

5. Study the exercise until you are prepared for dictation.

Lesson 36
(from Exercise 36, Weeds of Falsehood)

1. Read Exercise 36 in *Spelling Wisdom, Book 3*.

2. Parse and analyze the following sentence from the exercise.

   Some time ago a little boy told his first falsehood.

   Analyzing Tip: Keep in mind the three main patterns in a sentence:
   » *Sentence Pattern 1: Subject – Action Verb – Direct Object*
   » *Sentence Pattern 2: Subject – Linking Verb – Predicate Nominative (noun)*
   » *Sentence Pattern 3: Subject – Linking Verb – Predicate Adjective (adjective)*

3. Tell all you know about a simile.

   _____

   _____

4. Find two similes in the exercise and record them below.

   _____

   _____

   _____

   _____

5. Study the exercise until you are prepared for dictation.

Parse above the words:	PRO = pronoun	N = common noun	PN = proper noun	AV = action verb
	LV = linking verb	HV = helping verb	ADJ = adjective	ART = article
	ADV = adverb	PP = preposition	CON = conjunction	INT = interjection
Analyze below the words:	S = simple subject	P = simple predicate	DO = direct object	PN = predicate nominative
	PA = predicate adjective			

Lesson 37
(from Exercise 37, Out of Doors)

1. Read Exercise 37 in *Spelling Wisdom, Book 3.*

2. For each word listed below, find its antonym in the exercise.

   - different _____

   - cheerfulness _____

   - disappeared _____

   - apathy _____

   - ordinary _____

   - violent _____

   - dull _____

   - repulsive _____

   - agitation _____

   - abruptly _____

3. Look at the third sentence in Exercise 37. Why are the dashes there?

   _____

4. In the same sentence, why are the commas there?

   _____

5. Study the exercise until you are prepared for dictation.

Lesson 38
(from Exercise 38, Some Brief Memory)

1. Read Exercise 38 in *Spelling Wisdom, Book 3.*

2. Parse and analyze the following clause from the exercise.

   The boy stirred and smiled in his sleep

3. Are you ready for a challenge? Parse and analyze this long clause from the exercise. Hint: An object of a preposition cannot be the subject of a sentence.

   A strain of gentle music or the rippling of water in a silent place or the odor of a flower or the

   mention of a familiar word will sometimes call up sudden dim remembrances

    Analyzing Tip: *You will find it easier if you work through the mental process in order:*
   1. Find the verb and its subject. Narrow down the options by disregarding any modifiers.
   2. Look for the three main patterns (listed in Lesson 36).

4. The above clause has a compound _____.

5. Every prepositional phrase in that clause is modifying what part of speech and, therefore, doing what job?

   _____

6. Study the exercise until you are prepared for dictation.

Parse above the words:	PRO = pronoun	N = common noun	PN = proper noun	AV = action verb
	LV = linking verb	HV = helping verb	ADJ = adjective	ART = article
	ADV = adverb	PP = preposition	CON = conjunction	INT = interjection
Analyze below the words:	S = simple subject	P = simple predicate	DO = direct object	PN = predicate nominative
	PA = predicate adjective			

Lesson 39

(from Exercise 39, Equidistant Pennies)

1. Read Exercise 39 in *Spelling Wisdom, Book 3.*

2. Parse and analyze the following clause from the exercise. Now you get to learn something new about a subject: *here* and *there* can never be the subject of a clause. To discover the subject, say the verb and ask, "Who?" or "What?" For this clause, ask yourself, "Who or What <u>is</u>?"

   Here is a really hard puzzle

3. Now parse and analyze the following clause from Exercise 25.

   There was great food for meditation in this letter

    Writing Point: *As you learned in* Using Language Well, Book 2, *the verb and the subject should agree in number. Make sure that any sentences you write that begin with* here *or* there *base the verb on the true subject, not on those words. For example, "Here is your books" would be incorrect, because the true subject,* books, *is plural, and you would not say, "Books is here." The correct way to speak or write that sentence would be to make the verb match the true subject: "Here are your books."*

4. Use a dictionary to define *equidistant.*

_____

5. Can you solve the mathematics puzzle? Draw a diagram of the solution.

6. Study the exercise until you are prepared for dictation. Remember that the possessive *its* has no apostrophe.

Parse above the words:	PRO = pronoun	N = common noun	PN = proper noun	AV = action verb
	LV = linking verb	HV = helping verb	ADJ = adjective	ART = article
	ADV = adverb	PP = preposition	CON = conjunction	INT = interjection
Analyze below the words:	S = simple subject	P = simple predicate	DO = direct object	PN = predicate nominative
	PA = predicate adjective			

Lesson 40
(from Exercise 40, The Haircut)

1. Read Exercise 40 in *Spelling Wisdom, Book 3.*

2. Look through Exercises 1–40 and make note of the authors whose work was quoted in those exercises. Alphabetize those authors' names below, omitting duplicates. When alphabetizing names, arrange the entries by last name, then add the first name (and any other names given) at the end of each entry, preceded by a comma; for example, *Stevenson, Robert Louis.*

3. Study the exercise until you are prepared for dictation.

Lesson 41

(from Exercise 41, Trapping Words)

1. Read Exercise 41 in *Spelling Wisdom, Book 3.*

2. Parse and analyze the following clause from the exercise.

    I had now the key to all language

3. In the second sentence, why is the apostrophe after the *s* in *others'*?

    _____

    _____

4. Look back at Exercise 40. Why is the apostrophe before the *s* in *Emma's*?

    _____

    _____

5. What metaphor do you see in the second sentence of this exercise? Read the next two sentences to get the whole thought, then put the comparison in your own words.

    _____

    _____

    _____

    _____

6. Study the exercise until you are prepared for dictation.

Parse above the words: PRO = pronoun	N = common noun	PN = proper noun	AV = action verb
LV = linking verb	HV = helping verb	ADJ = adjective	ART = article
ADV = adverb	PP = preposition	CON = conjunction	INT = interjection
Analyze below the words: S = simple subject	P = simple predicate	DO = direct object	PN = predicate nominative
PA = predicate adjective			

Lesson 42
(from Exercise 42, Nature)

1. Read Exercise 42 in *Spelling Wisdom, Book 3.*

2. Remember how to read poetry so it makes the most sense? Read it slowly and be sure you're reading clause by clause. Don't automatically stop at the end of each line. Pause as punctuation dictates, not line breaks. Try to narrate the poem; put it in your own words.

    _____

    _____

    _____

    _____

3. See if you can figure out this poem's rhyme scheme.

    _____ over (Hint: In the original poem, the final word of this line is contracted to *o'er*.)

    _____ bed

    _____ led

    _____ floor

    _____ door

    _____ comforted

    _____ stead

    _____ more

    _____ away

    _____ hand

    _____ go

    _____ stay

    _____ understand

    _____ know

4. Now count the number of lines in the poem. _____

5. Do you recognize the pattern? What kind of poem is *Nature*? (Look back at Lesson 32 if you need help.)

    _____

    Writing Point: Remember that the scheme may change a bit according to the poet's style, but you can still recognize a sonnet for what it is.

6. Study the poem until you are prepared for dictation.

Lesson 43
(from Exercise 43, Fogg's Riches)

1. Read Exercise 43 in *Spelling Wisdom, Book 3.*

2. Parse and analyze the following sentence from the exercise.

   Was Phileas Fogg rich?

3. What do you notice about the order of words in that question? Which part of speech is out of its usual place?

   _____

4. Parse and analyze the following sentence from the exercise. Circle the parenthetical phrase and its punctuation.

   He was, in short, the least communicative of men.

   Record on page 153 the comma guideline that you have confirmed for parenthetical phrases.

5. Detail below the root word and suffixes of *undoubtedly*. Explain how each suffix changes the word's meaning or part of speech.
   - Root: _____
   - Suffix: _____
   - Suffix: _____

6. How does the prefix *un-* change the word's meaning?

   _____

7. Study the exercise until you are prepared for dictation.

Parse above the words:	PRO = pronoun	N = common noun	PN = proper noun	AV = action verb
	LV = linking verb	HV = helping verb	ADJ = adjective	ART = article
	ADV = adverb	PP = preposition	CON = conjunction	INT = interjection
Analyze below the words:	S = simple subject	P = simple predicate	DO = direct object	PN = predicate nominative
	PA = predicate adjective			

Lesson 44
(from Exercise 44, The Order of the Houses)

1. Read Exercise 44 in *Spelling Wisdom, Book 3.*

2. Look carefully at each mark of punctuation listed below and explain why it is used in the exercise. (If you need help, see Comma Guidelines on page 153.)

- "Let _____
- see," _____

_____

- line, _____
- "I _____
- here. _____
- Mortimer's _____
- tobacconist, _____
- shop, _____
- Bank, _____
- Restaurant, _____
- McFarlane's _____
- carriage-building _____
- now, _____
- Doctor, _____
- we've _____
- it's _____
- violin-land _____
- red-headed _____

3. Study the exercise until you are prepared for dictation.

Lesson 45
(from Exercise 45, Toothbrush and Nailbrush)

1. Read Exercise 45 in *Spelling Wisdom, Book 3.*

2. Parse and analyze the following sentence from the exercise. (Tip: *Such as* is considered a preposition in that sentence.)

   A more frequent application of a few utensils, such as soak toothbrush and nailbrush, might

   also be recommended to him!

   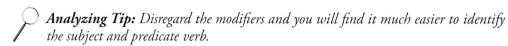 ***Analyzing Tip:*** *Disregard the modifiers and you will find it much easier to identify the subject and predicate verb.*

3. Why are the commas placed where they are in that sentence?

   _____

   _____

4. Tell what you know about a parenthetical phrase. (Look at Exercise 33 for help.)

   _____

   _____

5. As you have probably noticed in the exercises that you have written from dictation so far, exclamation points are used rarely. Why do you suppose Franz Liszt used one for the sentence above?

   _____

   _____

6. Study the exercise until you are prepared for dictation.

    Writing Point: *Sometimes a person's initials are substituted, in place of his full name, for discretion's sake. At other times initials are simply used as a shortcut, usually in informal writing.*

Parse above the words:	PRO = pronoun	N = common noun	PN = proper noun	AV = action verb
	LV = linking verb	HV = helping verb	ADJ = adjective	ART = article
	ADV = adverb	PP = preposition	CON = conjunction	INT = interjection
Analyze below the words:	S = simple subject	P = simple predicate	DO = direct object	PN = predicate nominative
	PA = predicate adjective			

Lesson 46
(from Exercise 46, Harvest on the Island)

1. Read Exercise 46 in *Spelling Wisdom, Book 3*.

2. In the exercise, find

   • an adjective prepositional phrase _____

   • an adverb prepositional phrase _____

   • a parenthetical expression _____

   • a hyphenated number _____

   • a number that is not hyphenated _____

   • a plural proper noun _____

   • a singular proper noun _____

3. Detail below the root word and suffixes of *plentifully*. Explain how each suffix changes the word's part of speech.

   • Root: _____

   • Suffix: _____

   • Suffix: _____

4. Study the exercise until you are prepared for dictation. Notice how *victualled* is spelled differently from the way it sounds: "vittled." (In modern spelling it has only one *l*, to read *victualed*.)

Lesson 47

(from Exercise 47, The Bicycle Salesman)

1. Read Exercise 47 in *Spelling Wisdom, Book 3*.

2. Parse and analyze the following clause from the exercise. (Remember what you learned about *here* and *there* in Lesson 39.)

   Here is a little tangle

3. Write two synonyms for each term listed below from the first sentence in the exercise. Check a thesaurus for helpful suggestions.
   - tangle _____ _____
   - perpetually _____ _____
   - cropping up _____ _____
   - guises _____ _____

4. Now rewrite the first sentence of the exercise in your own words.

   _____

   _____

   _____

5. Can you solve the mathematics puzzle? _____

6. Study the exercise until you are prepared for dictation. The British pound symbol officially looks like this: £. Exercise 47 uses a simple uppercase *L* instead. Feel free to use either when you write it, or you might use a cursive uppercase *L*. You might want to check the Internet (with adult supervision) to find out how a British pound compares to an American dollar.

Parse above the words:	PRO = pronoun	N = common noun	PN = proper noun	AV = action verb
	LV = linking verb	HV = helping verb	ADJ = adjective	ART = article
	ADV = adverb	PP = preposition	CON = conjunction	INT = interjection
Analyze below the words:	S = simple subject	P = simple predicate	DO = direct object	PN = predicate nominative
	PA = predicate adjective			

Lesson 48

(from Exercise 48, The Hat)

1. Read Exercise 48 in *Spelling Wisdom, Book 3.*

2. For each word given below, find its antonym in the exercise.

   • enemy _____

   • evening _____

   • insults _____

   • left _____

   • straightened _____

   • front _____

   • pristine _____

   • respectable _____

   • little _____

   • better _____

   • delineated _____

3. In the second sentence of the exercise, what is the group of words "evidently newly studied" called and what job is it doing?

   _____

   _____

4. Study the exercise until you are prepared for dictation.

Lesson 49
(from Exercise 49, Deduce)

1. Read Exercise 49 in *Spelling Wisdom, Book 3.*

2. Parse and analyze the following sentence from the exercise. (Remember what you learned about analyzing a question in Lesson 43.)

    "Did he not advertise?"

3. Is that group of words a clause or a phrase? How do you know?

    _____

    _____

4. You have learned about different types of phrases already. Now it is time to learn about types of clauses. An *independent* clause is a complete thought in itself. It can stand on its own. A *dependent* clause is not complete in itself but depends on another clause to complete the thought. Here are some independent clauses from previous exercises.

    The old men received Oliver with welcoming nods
    Dreams are the bright creatures of poem and legend
    Poverty certainly has not contracted her mind.
    External heat and cold had little influence on Scrooge.
    Was Phileas Fogg rich?

    What can you discover about independent clauses from the examples above? (For example, are they all sentences? Do they contain any phrases? See what you can notice on your own.)

    _____

    _____

    _____

5. Is the sentence that you parsed and analyzed in this lesson an independent or a dependent clause? How do you know?

    _____

    _____

6. Study the exercise until you are prepared for dictation.

Parse above the words:	PRO = pronoun	N = common noun	PN = proper noun	AV = action verb
	LV = linking verb	HV = helping verb	ADJ = adjective	ART = article
	ADV = adverb	PP = preposition	CON = conjunction	INT = interjection
Analyze below the words:	S = simple subject	P = simple predicate	DO = direct object	PN = predicate nominative
	PA = predicate adjective			

Lesson 50
(from Exercise 50, Changes)

1. Read Exercise 50 in *Spelling Wisdom, Book 3*.

2. Parse and analyze the following sentence from the exercise.

   Every time I come into this shrubbery I am more struck with its growth and beauty.

3. You should have found two subjects with their two corresponding predicate verbs, because that sentence is made up of two clauses put together. One is independent; the other is dependent. Here are some dependent clauses from previous exercises.

   When Edwards had secured his own boat
   who sport on earth in the night season
   if she had only a shilling in the world
   who will meet us and converse with us
   which no wealth could purchase or power bestow
   as soon as she was satisfied of her father's comfort
   as they were thus sitting together one day

   What can you discover about dependent clauses from the examples above? (For example, are any of them sentences? Look at the punctuation for that clue. Does the type of verb—action or linking—matter? Are the clauses missing something? See what you can notice on your own.)

   _____

   _____

   _____

4. Now look at the sentence you analyzed and parsed above. Identify the two clauses in it. Draw a straight line at either end of the independent clause, like this: | An independent clause expresses a complete thought in itself. |

   The dependent clause isn't complete in itself, so put an arrow at each end of it, like this: < whenever you mark a dependent clause >.

5. Study the exercise until you are prepared for dictation.

Parse above the words:	PRO = pronoun	N = common noun	PN = proper noun	AV = action verb
	LV = linking verb	HV = helping verb	ADJ = adjective	ART = article
	ADV = adverb	PP = preposition	CON = conjunction	INT = interjection
Analyze below the words:	S = simple subject	P = simple predicate	DO = direct object	PN = predicate nominative
	PA = predicate adjective			
Identify clauses:	| independent clause |	< dependent clause >		

Lesson 51

(from Exercise 51, Good Company)

1. Read Exercise 51 in *Spelling Wisdom, Book 3*.

2. Read the following clauses from previous exercises and determine whether each is dependent or independent. Draw a straight line at either end of an independent clause and an arrow at either end of a dependent clause.

    while there is infection in disease and sorrow

    God shall bring every work into judgment with every secret thing

    which no wealth could purchase or power bestow

    Mr. Crawford was considerably the best actor of all

    as far as she could judge

    who never hesitates at once to abandon an evil or questionable practice

    There was a frosty rime upon the trees

    I know not

    which meant that he gave great attention to details

    Mr. Pickwick took a seat and the paper

    who was an elderly, pimply-faced, vegetable-diet sort of man

    its power was only a glare

3. Look at the second sentence in Exercise 51. Explain why the dashes and the commas are in that sentence.

    _____

    _____

    _____

4. Study the exercise until you are prepared for dictation.

Identify clauses: | independent clause | < dependent clause >

Lesson 52
(from Exercise 52, To a Skylark)

1. Read Exercise 52 in *Spelling Wisdom, Book 3.*

2. What does *type* mean in the next to last line? Be sure to consider the context and all possible definitions.

   _____

3. Narrate the poem by explaining how the poet's skylark is a "type of the wise who soar, but never roam."

   _____

   _____

   _____

4. Let's take a look at the end rhymes of the poem. This one has an eye rhyme too. An *eye rhyme* is when two words look alike but sound different. The poet depends on the reader's eye to consider the two words as rhyming. Can you find the eye rhyme?

   _____

5. Now map out the poem's rhyme scheme.

   _____ sky

   _____ abound

   _____ eye

   _____ ground

   _____ will

   _____ still

   _____ wood

   _____ thine

   _____ flood

   _____ divine

   _____ roam

   _____ Home

   Writing Point: Though this rhyme scheme does not have a specific name, it is quite popular for a 6-line stanza or poem. You might try writing a poem of your own with that rhyme scheme.

6. That poem is not a sonnet. It is written in two sections, called stanzas. To analyze this poem, you could say that it has two _____-line stanzas with a rhyme scheme of _____.

7. Study the poem until you are prepared for dictation.

Lesson 53
(from Exercise 53, A New Coat for Father)

1. Read Exercise 53 in *Spelling Wisdom, Book 3*.

2. Parse and analyze the following sentence from the exercise. Be sure to mark dependent and independent clauses.

    With the very first pennies I make, I'll buy Father a new cloth coat.

3. You will find a word doing a new job in that sentence. First, make sure you found the direct object correctly. Say the subject and predicate verb and ask, "What?" "I'll buy (what?)." Pinocchio is not going to buy his father; he is going to buy a coat. The coat is the direct object, directly receiving the action of the verb. His father will receive some of the action indirectly, because the coat is for Father. So in this sentence, *Father* is doing the job of an *indirect object*.

    Mark the indirect object by writing *IO* below the word *Father*.

4. Now parse and analyze the following clause from Exercise 51. Be sure to mark whether it is an independent or dependent clause and also look for its indirect object. Hint: The indirect object will always come between the verb and the direct object. You can often confirm the indirect object by mentally inserting "to" or "for" in front of it.

    I do not promise you a good dinner

     Analyzing Tip: You will recall the three main patterns in a sentence. Keep in mind that sometimes an indirect object will be inserted between the action verb and the direct object, like this:
    » *Sentence Pattern 1: Subject – Action Verb – Direct Object*
                        Subject – Action Verb – (to or for) Indirect Object – Direct Object
    » *Sentence Pattern 2: Subject – Linking Verb – Predicate Nominative (noun)*
    » *Sentence Pattern 3: Subject – Linking Verb – Predicate Adjective (adjective)*

5. Study the exercise until you are prepared for dictation.

Parse above the words:	PRO = pronoun	N = common noun	PN = proper noun	AV = action verb
	LV = linking verb	HV = helping verb	ADJ = adjective	ART = article
	ADV = adverb	PP = preposition	CON = conjunction	INT = interjection
Analyze below the words:	S = simple subject	P = simple predicate	DO = direct object	IO = indirect object
	PN = predicate nominative	PA = predicate adjective		
Identify clauses:	| independent clause |	< dependent clause >		

Lesson 54

(from Exercise 54, Out of a Cave)

1. Read Exercise 54 in *Spelling Wisdom, Book 3*.

2. Parse and analyze the following excerpt from the exercise. Look for two short dependent clauses and one longer independent clause.

   if I stayed where I was, I should certainly one time or other be buried alive

    Analyzing Tip: *You will find it easier if you work through the mental process in order:*
   1. Find the verb and its subject. Narrow down the options by disregarding any modifiers.
   2. Look for the three main patterns (listed in Lesson 53).
   3. Identify the clauses. Each verb and its subject will be in a clause. Determine whether each clause is independent or dependent.

3. Now parse and analyze this excerpt from Exercise 51. Watch for the indirect object.

   It would give us great pleasure, my dear M. Brot, if you would come and dine with us

4. Why are the commas in the excerpt you parsed and analyzed in #3?

   _____

   _____

5. What job is the prepositional phrase doing in the dependent clause in #3?

   _____

   _____

6. Study the exercise until you are prepared for dictation.

Parse above the words:	PRO = pronoun	N = common noun	PN = proper noun	AV = action verb
	LV = linking verb	HV = helping verb	ADJ = adjective	ART = article
	ADV = adverb	PP = preposition	CON = conjunction	INT = interjection
Analyze below the words:	S = simple subject	P = simple predicate	DO = direct object	IO = indirect object
	PN = predicate nominative	PA = predicate adjective		
Identify clauses:	| independent clause |	< dependent clause >		

Lesson 55

(from Exercise 55, Admire the Scenery)

1. Read Exercise 55 in *Spelling Wisdom, Book 3*.

2. Parse and analyze the following sentence from the exercise. Be sure to mark the clause(s).

   By eleven o'clock the next day we were well upon our way to the old English capital.

3. Now parse and analyze the following excerpt, including the clause(s).

   there was an exhilarating nip in the air, which set an edge to a man's energy

4. Alphabetize the four proper nouns in Exercise 55.

   _____

   _____

   _____

   _____

5. Study the exercise until you are prepared for dictation.

Parse above the words:	PRO = pronoun	N = common noun	PN = proper noun	AV = action verb
	LV = linking verb	HV = helping verb	ADJ = adjective	ART = article
	ADV = adverb	PP = preposition	CON = conjunction	INT = interjection
Analyze below the words:	S = simple subject	P = simple predicate	DO = direct object	IO = indirect object
	PN = predicate nominative	PA = predicate adjective		
Identify clauses:	| independent clause |	< dependent clause >		

Lesson 56
(from Exercise 56, The Skipping-Rope)

1. Read Exercise 56 in *Spelling Wisdom, Book 3*.

2. Parse and analyze the following sentence from the exercise.

    She skipped down the walk toward him, and he lifted his head and looked at her with a curious

    expression.

 Analyzing Tip: *Go through this mental process:*
   1. Find the verb and its subject. Narrow down the options by disregarding any modifiers.
   2. Look for the three main patterns.
   3. Identify the clauses. Each verb and its subject will be in a clause.

3. Now parse and analyze this excerpt.

    She counted and skipped, and skipped and counted, until her cheeks were quite red

4. When a sentence contains two independent clauses, it is called a *compound sentence*. Usually two independent clauses are connected with a *coordinating conjunction: and, but, or, for, nor, so, yet.* Which of the two excerpts that you parsed and analyzed above (#2 or #3) would be considered a compound sentence? Why?

    _____

    _____

5. Identify the compound predicate verb in each of the two excerpts.

    _____

    _____

6. Study the exercise until you are prepared for dictation.

Parse above the words:	PRO = pronoun	N = common noun	PN = proper noun	AV = action verb
	LV = linking verb	HV = helping verb	ADJ = adjective	ART = article
	ADV = adverb	PP = preposition	CON = conjunction	INT = interjection
Analyze below the words:	S = simple subject	P = simple predicate	DO = direct object	IO = indirect object
	PN = predicate nominative	PA = predicate adjective		
Identify clauses:	| independent clause |	< dependent clause >		

Lesson 57

(from Exercise 57, Hot on the Trail)

1. Read Exercise 57 in *Spelling Wisdom, Book 3*.

2. Parse and analyze the following sentence from the exercise.

   Sherlock Holmes was transformed when he was hot upon such a scent as this.

3. Now try this sentence.

   His brows were drawn into two hard black lines, while his eyes shone out from beneath them with a steely glitter.

4. The next sentence in the exercise contains a simile. Find it and record it below.

   _____

   _____

5. Find the adjectives in the exercise that modify the two nouns below. Write the adjectives with their corresponding punctuation.

   _____ neck

   _____ snarl

6. Record on page 153 a comma guideline, summarizing what you see with those consecutive adjectives.

7. Study the exercise until you are prepared for dictation.

Parse above the words:	PRO = pronoun	N = common noun	PN = proper noun	AV = action verb
	LV = linking verb	HV = helping verb	ADJ = adjective	ART = article
	ADV = adverb	PP = preposition	CON = conjunction	INT = interjection
Analyze below the words:	S = simple subject	P = simple predicate	DO = direct object	IO = indirect object
	PN = predicate nominative	PA = predicate adjective		
Identify clauses:	| independent clause |	< dependent clause >		

simplycharlottemason.com

Lesson 58
(from Exercise 58, Looking for Boats)

1. Read Exercise 58 in *Spelling Wisdom, Book 3.*

2. Parse and analyze the following excerpt from the exercise.

    After I had thus laid the scheme of my design and in my imagination put it in practice, I continually made my tour every morning to the top of the hill

 Analyzing Tip: *Go through this mental process:*
1. Find the verb and its subject. Narrow down the options by disregarding any modifiers.
2. Look for the three main patterns.
3. Identify the clauses. Each verb and its subject will be in a clause.

3. What do you recall about a compound sentence? (Look back at Lesson 56 for help if you need it.)

    _____

    _____

    _____

4. A sentence with one independent clause and one (or more) dependent clauses is called a *complex sentence.* Is the excerpt that you parsed and analyzed above considered compound or complex? Why?

    _____

    _____

    _____

5. Study the exercise until you are prepared for dictation.

Parse above the words:	PRO = pronoun	N = common noun	PN = proper noun	AV = action verb
	LV = linking verb	HV = helping verb	ADJ = adjective	ART = article
	ADV = adverb	PP = preposition	CON = conjunction	INT = interjection
Analyze below the words:	S = simple subject	P = simple predicate	DO = direct object	IO = indirect object
	PN = predicate nominative	PA = predicate adjective		
Identify clauses:	| independent clause |	< dependent clause >		

Lesson 59
(from Exercise 59, Thunderstorm)

1. Read Exercise 59 in *Spelling Wisdom, Book 3*.

2. Parse and analyze the following excerpt from the exercise.

   It had been gradually getting overcast, and now the sky was dark and lowering

3. Is that excerpt compound or complex? Why?

   _____

   _____

4. Read the entire exercise again slowly, picturing each part of Dickens' description in your imagination. What part of his description is your favorite? Why?

   _____

   _____

   _____

   _____

5. Study the exercise until you are prepared for dictation.

Parse above the words:	PRO = pronoun	N = common noun	PN = proper noun	AV = action verb
	LV = linking verb	HV = helping verb	ADJ = adjective	ART = article
	ADV = adverb	PP = preposition	CON = conjunction	INT = interjection
Analyze below the words:	S = simple subject	P = simple predicate	DO = direct object	IO = indirect object
	PN = predicate nominative	PA = predicate adjective		
Identify clauses:	| independent clause |	< dependent clause >		

Lesson 60
(from Exercise 60, A Suit of Clothes)

1. Read Exercise 60 in *Spelling Wisdom, Book 3.*

2. For each word listed below, find a synonym from the exercise.

   - said _____

   - slew _____

   - quadruped _____

   - suitable _____

   - exterior _____

   - completely _____

   - hides _____

   - shirt _____

   - trousers _____

   - needing _____

   - admit _____

   - badly _____

3. Study the exercise until you are prepared for dictation.

Lesson 61

(from Exercise 61, August)

1. Read Exercise 61 in *Spelling Wisdom, Book 3.*

2. Parse and analyze the following sentence from the exercise.

   Spring has many beauties, and May is a fresh and blooming month, but the charms of this time of year are enhanced by their contrast with the winter season.

3. What kind of sentence is that: compound or complex? Why?

   _____

   _____

4. What job is the prepositional phrase, "of this time," doing in the last independent clause of that sentence?

   _____

5. Explain what the punctuation marks are doing in the next two sentences. Why is each one there?
   - advantage. _____
   - skies, _____
   - fields, _____
   - flowers— _____
   - earth— _____
   - is! _____

6. Study the exercise until you are prepared for dictation.

Parse above the words:	PRO = pronoun	N = common noun	PN = proper noun	AV = action verb
	LV = linking verb	HV = helping verb	ADJ = adjective	ART = article
	ADV = adverb	PP = preposition	CON = conjunction	INT = interjection
Analyze below the words:	S = simple subject	P = simple predicate	DO = direct object	IO = indirect object
	PN = predicate nominative	PA = predicate adjective		
Identify clauses:	| independent clause |	< dependent clause >		

simplycharlottemason.com

Lesson 62
(from Exercise 62, Statue of a Frenchman)

1. Read Exercise 62 in *Spelling Wisdom, Book 3.*

2. Define each word listed below, then, without looking at the exercise, determine which homonym from each set belongs in the given phrases.

   - knew _____

   - new _____

     the city of _____ **York**

   - time _____

   - thyme _____

     the _____ **of the Revolution**

   - right _____

   - write _____

     with his _____ **hand**

   - who's _____

   - whose _____

     _____ **memory is kept green**

3. Define each of the following words from the exercise, taking into account the context in which you find them. Use a dictionary if you need one.

   - bronze _____

   - noble _____

   - equestrian _____

   - gallant _____

   - devoted _____

   - fortune _____

   - green _____

4. Study the exercise until you are prepared for dictation.

Lesson 63
(from Exercise 63, Composed Upon Westminster Bridge)

1. Read Exercise 63 in *Spelling Wisdom, Book 3.*

2. Time for another poetry lesson. What does the title of the poem reveal to you? Where is that? What does the view look like? You might check the Internet (with an adult's supervision) to see what the poet saw in 1802.

   _____

   _____

3. Describe the tone of the poem and list the words or phrases that contribute to that tone.

   _____

   _____

4. Can you find the eye rhyme in it? _____

5. Analyze its rhyme scheme. What kind of poem is that; what name does it have? How do you know?

   _____

   _____

6. Another part of analyzing a poem is counting the number of syllables in each line. How many syllables does this poem have in each line?

   _____

   Writing Point: *The more you analyze poetry, the more you will understand how tricky it can be to write a good poem and the more you will appreciate those who do.*

7. Study the poem until you are prepared for dictation.

Lesson 64
(from Exercise 64, A Good Pastry Cook)

1. Read Exercise 64 in *Spelling Wisdom, Book 3*.

2. Parse and analyze the following excerpt from the exercise.

   When the firewood was burned pretty much into embers or live coals, I drew them forward

   upon this hearth

3. Would that excerpt be considered compound or complex? Why?

   _____

   _____

4. Now try the following excerpt and be sure to look for the indirect object.

   I made myself several cakes and puddings of the rice

5. What does *whelming* mean? Look up its definition, keeping in mind how it is used in the context of the passage.

   _____

   _____

6. Study the exercise until you are prepared for dictation.

Parse above the words:	PRO = pronoun	N = common noun	PN = proper noun	AV = action verb
	LV = linking verb	HV = helping verb	ADJ = adjective	ART = article
	ADV = adverb	PP = preposition	CON = conjunction	INT = interjection
Analyze below the words:	S = simple subject	P = simple predicate	DO = direct object	IO = indirect object
	PN = predicate nominative	PA = predicate adjective		
Identify clauses:	| independent clause |	< dependent clause >		

Lesson 65

(from Exercise 65, Paramount Importance)

1. Read Exercise 65 in *Spelling Wisdom, Book 3.*

2. Use a dictionary to look up the definition of each word below and record the one that best fits the context of the letter.

   • implicit _____

   • reliance _____

   • judgment _____

   • discretion _____

   • paramount _____

3. Compare this letter with the letter in Exercise 28. How would you describe the tone of each?

   _____

   _____

   _____

4. Now look closely at the punctuation at the end of their opening salutations. Summarize what you notice about the punctuation that should be used after the salutation of a formal letter versus an informal letter.

   _____

   _____

5. Study the exercise until you are prepared for dictation. Notice that the preferred spelling of *judgment* drops the *e* at the end of *judge* when adding the suffix *-ment*. (Both spellings are listed in the dictionary as correct, but the version listed first is the preferred spelling.)

Lesson 66

(from Exercise 66, Progress and Guessing)

1. Read Exercise 66 in *Spelling Wisdom, Book 3*.

2. Parse and analyze the following excerpt from the exercise.

   although we worked hard and faithfully, yet we did not quite reach our goal

3. Parse and analyze the following sentence too.

   I still regarded arithmetic as a system of pitfalls.

4. Look at the next sentence in the exercise and explain why the quotation marks are used.

   _____

   _____

5. Read the rest of the exercise and explain in your own words what Helen Keller meant by "the dangerous frontier of 'guess' " and "the broad valley of reason."

   _____

   _____

6. Study the exercise until you are prepared for dictation.

Parse above the words:	PRO = pronoun	N = common noun	PN = proper noun	AV = action verb
	LV = linking verb	HV = helping verb	ADJ = adjective	ART = article
	ADV = adverb	PP = preposition	CON = conjunction	INT = interjection
Analyze below the words:	S = simple subject	P = simple predicate	DO = direct object	IO = indirect object
	PN = predicate nominative	PA = predicate adjective		
Identify clauses:	| independent clause |	< dependent clause >		

Lesson 67

(from Exercise 67, God Employs Little Things)

1. Read Exercise 67 in *Spelling Wisdom, Book 3.*

2. Parse and analyze the following sentence from the exercise.

    Look at yonder sun.

     Analyzing Tip: *Go through this mental process:*
    1. Find the verb and its subject. Narrow down the options by disregarding any modifiers.
    2. Look for the three main patterns.
    3. Identify the clauses. Each verb and its subject will be in a clause.

3. Now parse and analyze the sentence below.

    God made it and hung it up there in the sky that it might give light to our world.

4. What kind of sentence is #3: compound or complex? Why?

    _____

    _____

5. What does *employs* mean in the context of the exercise? Use a dictionary to help you if needed.

    _____

    _____

6. Study the exercise until you are prepared for dictation.

Parse above the words:	PRO = pronoun	N = common noun	PN = proper noun	AV = action verb
	LV = linking verb	HV = helping verb	ADJ = adjective	ART = article
	ADV = adverb	PP = preposition	CON = conjunction	INT = interjection
Analyze below the words:	S = simple subject	P = simple predicate	DO = direct object	IO = indirect object
	PN = predicate nominative	PA = predicate adjective		
Identify clauses:	| independent clause |	< dependent clause >		

simplycharlottemason.com

Lesson 68
(from Exercise 68, Agree in Number)

1. Read Exercise 68 in *Spelling Wisdom, Book 3.*

2. Parse and analyze the following sentence from the exercise.

   It sounds somewhat intimidating, but it really is easy if you only think about it.

3. Is that sentence compound or complex? _____

   If you answer "both," you are correct. It has two independent clauses joined by a coordinating conjunction: *but*. It also has an dependent clause attached with *if* (which is a subordinating conjunction). So this sentence would be called a *compound-complex sentence*. It is both!

4. Look up the definitions of the two words below when each is used as an **adjective**.

   - coordinate _____

   - subordinate _____

5. Using what you learned from the dictionary definitions, explain why independent clauses are joined by a coordinating conjunction and dependent clauses are attached with subordinate conjunctions.

   _____

   _____

   _____

   _____

   Writing Point: *You will find lists of common coordinating conjunctions and subordinating conjunctions on page 155. Get familiar with them so you can use a wide range in your writing.*

6. Study the exercise until you are prepared for dictation.

Parse above the words:	PRO = pronoun	N = common noun	PN = proper noun	AV = action verb
	LV = linking verb	HV = helping verb	ADJ = adjective	ART = article
	ADV = adverb	PP = preposition	CON = conjunction	INT = interjection
Analyze below the words:	S = simple subject	P = simple predicate	DO = direct object	IO = indirect object
	PN = predicate nominative	PA = predicate adjective		
Identify clauses:	| independent clause |	< dependent clause >		

Lesson 69

(from Exercise 69, Thanks for the Harvest)

1. Read Exercise 69 in *Spelling Wisdom, Book 3*.

2. Parse and analyze the following sentence from the exercise.

    We may not be altogether satisfied with the year's results, and we can do a terrific amount of grumbling when we take the notion.

3. Tell what you know about compound, complex, and compound-complex sentences (including their conjunctions) and identify which one the above sentence is.

    _____

    _____

    _____

    _____

    _____

4. List below the two conjunctions that begin clauses in that sentence and identify whether each one is coordinating or subordinating. (Use the lists on page 155 to help you if needed.)

    _____

5. Tell all you know about direct objects and indirect objects. Give a sample sentence that includes both and identify them.

    _____

    _____

    _____

    _____

    _____

6. Study the exercise until you are prepared for dictation.

Parse above the words:	PRO = pronoun	N = common noun	PN = proper noun	AV = action verb
	LV = linking verb	HV = helping verb	ADJ = adjective	ART = article
	ADV = adverb	PP = preposition	CON = conjunction	INT = interjection
Analyze below the words:	S = simple subject	P = simple predicate	DO = direct object	IO = indirect object
	PN = predicate nominative	PA = predicate adjective		
Identify clauses:	| independent clause |	< dependent clause >		

Lesson 70
(from Exercise 70, The Ocean Course)

1. Read Exercise 70 in *Spelling Wisdom, Book 3.*

2. Parse and analyze the following sentence from the exercise.

   The polar circle was soon passed, and the course shaped for Cape Horn.

3. Underline the prepositional phrase in the sentence you parsed. Write here the job it is doing and the word it modifies.

   _____

4. Explain the difference between a phrase and a clause.

   _____

   _____

5. What do you know about subject complements? Tell in full.

   _____

   _____

   _____

   _____

   _____

6. Notice the first word in the first two sentences of the exercise. What part of speech are those words?

   _____

7. Study the exercise until you are prepared for dictation.

Parse above the words:	PRO = pronoun	N = common noun	PN = proper noun	AV = action verb
	LV = linking verb	HV = helping verb	ADJ = adjective	ART = article
	ADV = adverb	PP = preposition	CON = conjunction	INT = interjection
Analyze below the words:	S = simple subject	P = simple predicate	DO = direct object	IO = indirect object
	PN = predicate nominative	PA = predicate adjective		
Identify clauses:	| independent clause |	< dependent clause >		

Lesson 71
(from Exercise 71, Journey Mercies)

1. Read Exercise 71 in *Spelling Wisdom, Book 3.*

2. Parse and analyze the following sentence from the exercise.

    The poor Indians appeared very glad of my return.

3. Underline the prepositional phrase and tell what job it is doing and what word it modifies.

    _____

4. Parse and analyze the sentence below.

    Found my house and all things in safety.

5. Is that sentence simple, compound, complex, or compound-complex? (A simple sentence is comprised of a single independent clause.)

    _____

6. That sentence has a compound _____ in it.

7. Study the exercise until you are prepared for dictation.

Parse above the words:	PRO = pronoun	N = common noun	PN = proper noun	AV = action verb
	LV = linking verb	HV = helping verb	ADJ = adjective	ART = article
	ADV = adverb	PP = preposition	CON = conjunction	INT = interjection
Analyze below the words:	S = simple subject	P = simple predicate	DO = direct object	IO = indirect object
	PN = predicate nominative	PA = predicate adjective		
Identify clauses:	| independent clause |	< dependent clause >		

Lesson 72
(from Exercise 72, Courteous to Aunts)

1. Read Exercise 72 in *Spelling Wisdom, Book 3*.

2. Parse and analyze the following clause from the exercise.

   you will be sure

3. If you look at the next phrase in the sentence, you will discover another part of speech that can modify.

   you will be sure to find a tender welcome

   You have seen prepositional phrases do the jobs of adjective and adverb, but the phrase "to find a tender welcome" is not a prepositional phrase. If it said, "you will be sure *of a tender welcome*," that would be a prepositional phrase. Why is "to find a tender welcome" not a prepositional phrase?

   _____

4. Verbs usually show action in a sentence or link subjects and their complements together, but verbs can take different forms and do other jobs too. In the upcoming lessons, you will meet three different verb forms (also called *verbals*) that can do other jobs.

   This exercise contains the first: an *infinitive*. In the phrase, "to find a tender welcome," the two words *to find* are the infinitive. What word in the clause (#3) is that infinitive phrase modifying?

   _____

   So it is doing what job? _____

5. An infinitive will almost always have *to* in front of the verb: "to (verb)." Label the infinitive in #3 by writing —*inf*— above its words.

6. Study the exercise until you are prepared for dictation.

Parse above the words:	PRO = pronoun	N = common noun	PN = proper noun	AV = action verb
	LV = linking verb	HV = helping verb	ADJ = adjective	ART = article
	ADV = adverb	PP = preposition	CON = conjunction	INT = interjection
	—inf— = infinitive			
Analyze below the words:	S = simple subject	P = simple predicate	DO = direct object	IO = indirect object
	PN = predicate nominative	PA = predicate adjective		
Identify clauses:	| independent clause |	< dependent clause >		

Lesson 73

(from Exercise 73, Breathes There the Man)

1. Read Exercise 73 in *Spelling Wisdom, Book 3*.

2. You already know about rhyme in poetry. What is the rhyme scheme for the poem in this exercise?

   _____

3. Poetry also has rhythm, or *meter*, a repeating pattern like the beat in music. Each unit of that rhythm is called a *foot*. The poem in Exercise 73 has a two-syllable foot. Each group of two syllables forms a rhythm that moves the poem along.

   Try reading the first line aloud, putting the accent on the first syllable of each foot:

   BREATHES there / THE man, / WITH soul / SO dead.

   Not very smooth. Now switch it and try reading with the stress on the second syllable of each foot:

   Breathes THERE / the MAN, / with SOUL / so DEAD

   Much smoother. A two-syllable foot, in which the second syllable is stressed, is called an *iambic* foot. That's because each group of two syllables in that type of foot is called an *iamb*. How many iambs do you see in that first line of the poem?

   _____

   Writing Point: You may notice that some of the lines of the poem in this exercise have an extra syllable. It is in those places that the poet originally used a contraction to abbreviate a word and preserve the iambic foot. Now you know why you sometimes see unusual contractions in poetry, such as ne'er and wand'ring. In Spelling Wisdom, many of those contractions have been removed and replaced with the entire word in order to make sure you learn how to spell the longer, more commonly-used form correctly.

4. Enough about analyzing. Let's focus on the powerful patriotic words. Read the poem again, then look up the definitions of the words below to help you understand the poet's ideas.

   • pelf _____

   • concentered _____

   • renown _____

5. What do you think Sir Walter Scott meant by "doubly dying"?

   _____

   _____

6. What would you say is the main idea of this poem? What was Scott seeking to communicate?

   _____

   _____

7. Study the poem until you are prepared for dictation.

Lesson 74
(from Exercise 74, Why Is the World So Beautiful if Not for Us?)

1. Read Exercise 74 in *Spelling Wisdom, Book 3*.

2. Parse and analyze the following sentence from the exercise.

   Have you noticed the wonderful coloring of the sky at sunrise?

3. Explain what *personification* means. (Check Lessons 31 and 34 if you need help.)

   _____

   _____

4. Find the sentence that uses personification in the exercise and explain it.

   _____

   _____

5. Tell what an infinitive is. (Look back at Lesson 72 for help.)

   _____

   _____

6. Find the infinitive in the following clause from Exercise 21. Label it *—inf—* above the words.

   she was glad to leave him

7. Explain what word the infinitive phrase is modifying in the clause and what job it is doing.

   _____

8. Study the exercise until you are prepared for dictation.

Parse above the words:	PRO = pronoun	N = common noun	PN = proper noun	AV = action verb
	LV = linking verb	HV = helping verb	ADJ = adjective	ART = article
	ADV = adverb	PP = preposition	CON = conjunction	INT = interjection
	—inf— = infinitive			
Analyze below the words:	S = simple subject	P = simple predicate	DO = direct object	IO = indirect object
	PN = predicate nominative	PA = predicate adjective		
Identify clauses:	| independent clause |	< dependent clause >		

Lesson 75

(from Exercise 75, Love of Money)

1. Read Exercise 75 in *Spelling Wisdom, Book 3.*

2. Parse the following sentence from the exercise. Don't analyze it until later.

    I want to congratulate you on your receipt of such a large sum of money.

3. Did you find the infinitive? You have previously seen that infinitives can do the job of modifiers. But infinitives can also do jobs that nouns can do in a sentence, such as the job of subject or direct object. In the sentence that you parsed, the infinitive is doing the job of direct object. You can tell by saying the subject and the predicate verb, then asking, "What?"—"I want (<u>what?</u>)" The answer to that question is the direct object of the sentence. Analyze the sentence in #2. (You'll need to extend lines out from your *DO* label in order to indicate that the entire infinitive phrase, "to congratulate you," is the direct object in that sentence.)

4. Parse and analyze the following sentence from Exercise 44. Look for the infinitive and pay special attention to what job the infinitive phrase is doing.

    I should like just to remember the order of the houses here.

5. Now parse and analyze the following sentence from Exercise 57.

    Men who had only known the quiet thinker and logician of Baker Street would have failed to

    recognize him.

6. Tell whether the conjunction that begins the dependent clause in that sentence is coordinating or subordinating. (Use the lists on page 155 to help you if needed.)

7. Study the exercise until you are prepared for dictation.

Parse above the words:	PRO = pronoun	N = common noun	PN = proper noun	AV = action verb
	LV = linking verb	HV = helping verb	ADJ = adjective	ART = article
	ADV = adverb	PP = preposition	CON = conjunction	INT = interjection
	—inf— = infinitive			
Analyze below the words:	S = simple subject	P = simple predicate	DO = direct object	IO = indirect object
	PN = predicate nominative	PA = predicate adjective		
Identify clauses:	| independent clause |	< dependent clause >		

Lesson 76
(from Exercise 76, First Thing in The Morning)

1. Read Exercise 76 in *Spelling Wisdom, Book 3.*

2. What do you know about similes and metaphors?

   _____

   _____

   _____

3. Find the metaphor in the exercise and explain it.

   _____

   _____

   _____

4. Find the simile in the exercise and explain it.

   _____

   _____

   _____

5. Parse and analyze the following clause from the exercise. Be sure to look for the infinitive.

   Satan will attempt to fill it with worldly cares or fleshly desires

   Analyzing Tip: Be sure to use the three-step process when analyzing a sentence. (See Lesson 67.) If the infinitive is acting as a modifier, you can disregard it along with the other modifiers. But if it is acting as a noun, keep it in mind when you look for the three main patterns.

6. That clause has a compound _____.

7. Study the exercise until you are prepared for dictation.

Parse above the words:	PRO = pronoun	N = common noun	PN = proper noun	AV = action verb
	LV = linking verb	HV = helping verb	ADJ = adjective	ART = article
	ADV = adverb	PP = preposition	CON = conjunction	INT = interjection
	—inf— = infinitive			
Analyze below the words:	S = simple subject	P = simple predicate	DO = direct object	IO = indirect object
	PN = predicate nominative	PA = predicate adjective		
Identify clauses:	| independent clause |	< dependent clause >		

Lesson 77

(from Exercise 77, The Name on the Shield)

1. Read Exercise 77 in *Spelling Wisdom, Book 3.*

2. Define each word listed below; then, without looking at the exercise, determine which homonym from each set belongs in the given statement.

   • there _____

   • they're _____

   • their _____

      Men have been very ingenious in trying to find out ways by which _____

      names might be remembered among men when they themselves have passed away.

3. Look closely at the following two sentences from previous exercises. What two things separate the independent clauses within each sentence? Look at both punctuation and parts of speech.

   _____ and _____

      We may not be altogether satisfied with the year's results, and we can do a terrific amount of grumbling when we take the notion.

      I could not answer that question, and I feared that Captain Nemo would rather take us to the vast ocean that touches the coasts of Asia and America at the same time.

4. Now look closely at the final sentence of Exercise 77. You will find several independent clauses within it. What is separating them?

   _____

5. Compare those independent clauses with the ones you looked at in #3. What is different? What is missing?

   _____

6. Based on your observations, write two guidelines below for punctuating independent clauses within a sentence.

   _____

   _____

   _____

   Writing Point: *Did you notice how the final sentence in Exercise 77 repeats the same phrase, "is gone," in three clauses? Repetition can provide emphasis on a key idea. Too much repetition, however, can be a sign of carelessness. Make sure you use repetition intentionally in your writing.*

7. Study the exercise until you are prepared for dictation.

Lesson 78

(from Exercise 78, Day of the Week)

1. Read Exercise 78 in *Spelling Wisdom, Book 3*.

2. Parse and analyze the following clause from the exercise.

   He therefore decided to test the fellow's intelligence

3. Tell what an infinitive is. (Did you find the one in the sentence you parsed above?)

   _____

   _____

4. You have seen that an infinitive can do two jobs: the job of a modifier or of a noun. The other two verb forms, or verbals, that you need to know about also do those two jobs, but they are limited to only one job each. In this lesson, let's talk about a *participle*. A participle acts only as a modifier. You can tell it apart from an infinitive quite easily, because a participle usually ends in *-ing* or *-ed*, whereas the infinitive starts with *to* ___. Find the participle in the first sentence of Exercise 78. Just look for the *-ing* verb that is modifying the noun, *yokel*.

   _____

   Since that verb form is doing the work of a modifier, it is called a participle.

5. Parse and analyze the first sentence of Exercise 78 (given below) and mark the participle with *par*.

   A facetious individual who was taking a long walk in the country came upon a yokel sitting on

   a stile.

6. Tell whether the conjunction that begins the dependent clause in that sentence is coordinating or subordinating. (Use the lists on page 155 to help you if needed.)

   _____

7. Can you figure out what day of the week it was? _____

8. Study the exercise until you are prepared for dictation.

Parse above the words:	PRO = pronoun	N = common noun	PN = proper noun	AV = action verb
	LV = linking verb	HV = helping verb	ADJ = adjective	ART = article
	ADV = adverb	PP = preposition	CON = conjunction	INT = interjection
	—inf— = infinitive	par = participle		
Analyze below the words:	S = simple subject	P = simple predicate	DO = direct object	IO = indirect object
	PN = predicate nominative	PA = predicate adjective		
Identify clauses:	| independent clause |	< dependent clause >		

Lesson 79

(from Exercise 79, The Grindstone)

1. Read Exercise 79 in *Spelling Wisdom, Book 3.*

2. Use the chart below to explain the jobs that the two verb forms you've studied so far can do.

Verbal	Form	Job
Participle	-ing *or* -ed	_____
Infinitive	to ____	_____
	to ____	_____

3. Parse and analyze the following sentence from the exercise.

   This machine cost me a full week's work to bring it to perfection.

4. Why is *to perfection* not considered an infinitive?

   _____

   _____

5. Now parse and analyze the following excerpt from Exercise 56. Look for two participles (joined with a conjunction to form a compound participle).

   She skipped at last into the kitchen garden and saw Ben Weatherstaff digging and talking to his

   robin

6. What word(s) is the participial phrase modifying?

   _____

7. Study the exercise until you are prepared for dictation.

Parse above the words:	PRO = pronoun	N = common noun	PN = proper noun	AV = action verb
	LV = linking verb	HV = helping verb	ADJ = adjective	ART = article
	ADV = adverb	PP = preposition	CON = conjunction	INT = interjection
	—inf— = infinitive	par = participle		
Analyze below the words:	S = simple subject	P = simple predicate	DO = direct object	IO = indirect object
	PN = predicate nominative	PA = predicate adjective		
Identify clauses:	| independent clause |	< dependent clause >		

 simplycharlottemason.com

Lesson 80

(from Exercise 80, Horse Owners)

1. Read Exercise 80 in *Spelling Wisdom, Book 3*.

2. Parse and analyze the following excerpt from the exercise and look for the infinitive. (Remember what you learned about *here* and *there* as a subject.)

   There are good thoughtful men like our master, that any horse may be proud to serve.

3. Did you notice how many modifiers are in that excerpt? For each modifier listed below, write the word it is modifying.

Modifier	Word It Is Modifying
Good	_____
Thoughtful	_____
Like our master	_____
Any	_____
To serve	_____

4. In fact, the entire dependent clause is modifying a word in the independent clause. Can you find it?

   _____

5. What part of speech is the word that it is modifying? _____

   Would that dependent clause be considered an adjective clause or an adverb clause?

   _____

   Writing Point: Adjective clauses usually start with who, whom, whose, which, *and* that. *Use* who, whom, *and* whose *when modifying people. Use* which *and* that *when modifying things.*

6. Study the exercise until you are prepared for dictation.

Parse above the words:	PRO = pronoun	N = common noun	PN = proper noun	AV = action verb
	LV = linking verb	HV = helping verb	ADJ = adjective	ART = article
	ADV = adverb	PP = preposition	CON = conjunction	INT = interjection
	—inf— = infinitive	par = participle		
Analyze below the words:	S = simple subject	P = simple predicate	DO = direct object	IO = indirect object
	PN = predicate nominative	PA = predicate adjective		
Identify clauses:	| independent clause |	< dependent clause >		

Lesson 81
(from Exercise 81, What the Sun Saw)

1. Read Exercise 81 in *Spelling Wisdom, Book 3*.

2. Tell what you know about infinitives and participles.

_____

_____

_____

_____

3. The final verb form that you need to know is the *gerund*. It is similar to a participle, in that it usually has an *-ing* ending, but a gerund does the job of a noun. It might act as the subject, the direct object, or an object of a preposition in a sentence. Whatever a noun can do, a gerund can do.

   As you parse and analyze the following clause from the exercise, look closely for the gerund that is acting as an object of a preposition. Label the gerund with *ger*. (You'll find an infinitive too, just for good measure.)

   Amy had capped the climax by putting a clothespin on her nose to uplift the offending feature

4. Now parse and analyze the following clause from Exercise 69. Look for a compound gerund that is the object of a preposition.

   the rush and struggle of growing and saving the crops is past for another year

5. Both the first sentence and the last sentence of Exercise 81 contain a possessive word. One has the apostrophe before the *s*; the other has the apostrophe after the *s*. Write the two possessive words below and explain why each has the apostrophe where it is.

_____

_____

6. Study the exercise until you are prepared for dictation.

Parse above the words:	PRO = pronoun	N = common noun	PN = proper noun	AV = action verb
	LV = linking verb	HV = helping verb	ADJ = adjective	ART = article
	ADV = adverb	PP = preposition	CON = conjunction	INT = interjection
	—inf— = infinitive	par = participle	ger = gerund	
Analyze below the words:	S = simple subject	P = simple predicate	DO = direct object	IO = indirect object
	PN = predicate nominative	PA = predicate adjective		
Identify clauses:	| independent clause |	< dependent clause >		

Lesson 82
(from Exercise 82, Rip Van Winkle's Dog)

1. Read Exercise 82 in *Spelling Wisdom, Book 3*.

2. Parse and analyze the following clause from the exercise. Watch for a participle.

   he sneaked about with a gallows air, casting many a sidelong glance at Dame Van Winkle

3. Since participles are modifiers, they must modify something. What word in that clause is the participial phrase modifying?

   _____

   ✎ ***Writing Point:*** *Make sure any participle in your writing modifies another word in the sentence. If you cannot pinpoint the word it modifies, rewrite the sentence.*

4. Now parse and analyze the following excerpt from Exercise 34.

   The fire glows brightly, crackling with a sharp and cheerful sound

5. Try the following clause from Exercise 41. Look for the gerund.

   Gradually from naming an object we advance step by step

6. Remember, a gerund does the job of a noun. What job is the gerund phrase doing in the clause you just analyzed?

   _____

   _____

7. What did the author of Exercise 82 mean by using the term "a gallows air"? What was he trying to communicate about the dog's situation and manner?

   _____

   _____

8. Study the exercise until you are prepared for dictation.

Parse above the words:	PRO = pronoun	N = common noun	PN = proper noun	AV = action verb
	LV = linking verb	HV = helping verb	ADJ = adjective	ART = article
	ADV = adverb	PP = preposition	CON = conjunction	INT = interjection
	—inf— = infinitive	par = participle	ger = gerund	
Analyze below the words:	S = simple subject	P = simple predicate	DO = direct object	IO = indirect object
	PN = predicate nominative	PA = predicate adjective		
Identify clauses:	| independent clause |	< dependent clause >		

Lesson 83
(from Exercise 83, Daffodils)

1. Read Exercise 83 in *Spelling Wisdom, Book 3.*

2. The first step to take with a poem is to make sure you understand what ideas the poet was communicating. Summarize each stanza of the poem in one sentence.

    Stanza 1: _____

    _____

    Stanza 2: _____

    _____

    Stanza 3: _____

    _____

    Stanza 4: _____

    _____

3. Look up the possible definitions of the two italicized words in the lines from the poem below and determine which definition fits best, keeping the context of the clause and the poem in mind. Then rewrite the two lines in your own words, staying true to the poet's original meaning. (Your paraphrase does not need to rhyme, but it may if you would like to try.)

    A poet could not but be *gay*
    In such a *jocund* company

    _____

    _____

4. Now analyze the poem as outlined below.
    - Number of stanzas _____
    - Lines per stanza _____
    - Rhyme scheme _____
    - List any eye rhymes _____
    - Syllables per line _____
    - Syllables per foot _____
    - Number of foot per line _____
    - Accent on which syllable of the foot? _____

    Do you recall what that type of foot is called? (Check Lesson 73 for a reminder.)

5. Study the poem until you are prepared for dictation.

Lesson 84
(from Exercise 84, The Building)

1. Read Exercise 84 in *Spelling Wisdom, Book 3*.

2. Detail below the differences between the three verbals you have learned about.

Verbal	Form	Job
Gerund	_____	_____
Participle	_____	_____
Infinitive	_____	_____
	_____	_____

3. Find the simile in the first sentence of the exercise. _____

4. Find the participle in the third sentence, modifying *smoke*. _____

5. How many independent clauses are in the fourth sentence of the exercise and what guideline has been used to separate them? Record that guideline on page 153.

6. Why is there no comma before each *and* in the final sentence?

    up and down _____

    lawn and examined _____

7. Study the exercise until you are prepared for dictation.

Lesson 85

(from Exercise 85, Forego and Give Up)

1. Read Exercise 85 in *Spelling Wisdom, Book 3.*

2. For each modifier listed below—whether a single word, a phrase, or a dependent clause—list the word(s) from the exercise that it is modifying and whether it is doing the job of an adjective or an adverb.

Modifier	Word Modified	Adjective or Adverb
that I can do		
for the sake of peace		
stumbling		
to others		
cheerfully		
to him		
on my knees		
he has done me		
of my humble confession		
as the only person guilty		

3. What did the author mean when he wrote, "I feel disposed"? Check a dictionary to discover the possible definitions for that word and select the best one for the context of the passage.

_____

_____

4. Study the exercise until you are prepared for dictation.

Lesson 86
(from Exercise 86, Distribute One Million)

1. Read Exercise 86 in *Spelling Wisdom, Book 3*.

2. Find the participial phrase that is modifying *Mr. Morgan G. Bloomgarten*. (Look carefully. That participle does not end in *ing* or *ed*, but it is a verb form that is doing the job of modifying, so it is a participle.)

   _____

3. The first sentence of the exercise also contains an appositive for *Mr. Morgan G. Bloomgarten*. An *appositive* is a noun or pronoun that explains or renames the preceding noun or pronoun. Think of it as the author's giving more information to clarify exactly what or whom he is writing about. What is the appositive in that first sentence of the exercise?

   _____

4. Find the appositives for the words listed below in previous exercises.

Exercise	Word or Phrase	Appositive
48	*my friend*	_____
51	*tomorrow*	_____
82	*his dog*	_____

5. How would you distribute the money as outlined in the exercise?

   _____

   _____

   _____

6. Study the exercise until you are prepared for dictation.

Lesson 87
(from Exercise 87, Psalm 32)

1. Read Exercise 87 in *Spelling Wisdom, Book 3.*

2. For each dependent clause listed below, tell the word from the exercise that it is modifying and, therefore, what kind of dependent clause it is: adjective or adverb.

Clause	Word Modified	Adjective or Adverb
Whose trangression is forgiven		
Whose sin is covered		
When I kept silence		
That is godly		
When thou mayest be found		
Which thou shalt go		
Which have no understanding		
That trusteth in the Lord		

3. The following words from the exercise have suffixes. Detail each one's root word and how its suffix has changed its part of speech.

   transgression

   Root: _____

   Change: _____

   surely

   Root: _____

   Change: _____

   deliverance

   Root: _____

   Change: _____

4. Find the simile in the exercise and explain what it is comparing.

   _____

   _____

5. Study the exercise until you are prepared for dictation. Remember that a psalm is a song. The word *Selah* is probably a musical term that meant to pause and give the singers and listeners time to think about what was just said.

Lesson 88

(from Exercise 88, Mud Spatters)

1. Read Exercise 88 in *Spelling Wisdom, Book 3*.

2. Parse and analyze the following sentence from the exercise.

   The lady gave a violent start and stared in bewilderment at my companion.

3. Why is no comma needed before "and stared"?

   _____

   _____

4. For each dependent clause listed below, tell the word from the exercise that it is modifying and whether it is acting as an adjective or an adverb.

Dependent Clause	Modifies	Adjective or Adverb
before you reached the station	_____	_____
which throws up mud in that way	_____	_____

5. What kind of verbal do you find in the first sentence of the exercise: an infinitive, a participle, or a gerund? Explain how you know it is that kind of verbal.

   _____

   _____

6. Find the interjection in the third paragraph of the exercise and notice what punctuation is paired with it. Now look back at a similar sentence in Exercise 53 (the seventh sentence) and see if it has similar punctuation.

   _____

   Record on page 153 the guideline you have discovered.

7. Study the exercise until you are prepared for dictation.

Parse above the words:	PRO = pronoun	PN = proper noun	AV = action verb
	LV = linking verb	ADJ = adjective	ART = article
	ADV = adverb	CON = conjunction	INT = interjection
	—inf— = infinitive	ger = gerund	

Additional entries: N = common noun, HV = helping verb, PP = preposition, par = participle.

Analyze below the words:	S = simple subject	DO = direct object	IO = indirect object
	PN = predicate nominative		

Additional: P = simple predicate, PA = predicate adjective

Identify clauses:	| independent clause | < dependent clause >

Lesson 89

(from Exercise 89, Provisions)

1. Read Exercise 89 in *Spelling Wisdom, Book 3.*

2. For each word listed below, find its antonym in the exercise.

   • conclusion _____

   • disagreeable _____

   • regularly _____

   • requests _____

   • unnaturally _____

   • successes _____

   • cruelly _____

   • luck _____

3. What does *essays* mean in the context of the exercise? Use a dictionary to help you.

   _____

4. What two meanings can the word *wanted* have?

   _____

   _____

5. Which of those meanings do you think is intended in the exercise? Why?

   _____

   _____

6. Study the exercise until you are prepared for dictation.

Lesson 90
(from Exercise 90, The Historian's Responsibility)

1. Read Exercise 90 in *Spelling Wisdom, Book 3*.

2. Alphabetize the following words from the exercise.

origin   _____

rise   _____

advanced   _____

retarded   _____

sought   _____

sentiments   _____

prevailed   _____

civil   _____

philosophy   _____

prevails   _____

ascertained   _____

literature   _____

religion   _____

industrial   _____

agriculture   _____

commerce   _____

cultivator   _____

peasant   _____

prayers   _____

prayed   _____

connected   _____

war   _____

wrought   _____

weapons   _____

organized   _____

3. Study the exercise until you are prepared for dictation.

Lesson 91

(from Exercise 91, Robin Quarrels)

1. Read Exercise 91 in *Spelling Wisdom, Book 3*.

2. Parse and analyze the following sentence from the exercise. Watch for the participle.

   One pair built their nest for three summers in a basket suspended from the ceiling of my front piazza, where people were constantly coming and going.

3. For each phrase or clause given below, tell what it modifies.

   for three summers _____

   in a basket _____

   suspended from the ceiling _____

   of my front piazza _____

   where people were constantly coming and going _____

4. How would the sentence's meaning change if one of the modifiers were moved to a different place? Read these rearrangements and note the different idea each one communicates.

   One pair built their nest for three summers where people were constantly coming and going in a basket suspended from the ceiling of my front piazza.

   _____

   One pair, suspended from the ceiling of my front piazza, built their nest for three summers where people in a basket were constantly coming and going.

   _____

5. Based on those rearrangements, what guideline about modifiers can you create to help with your own writing? Where should modifiers be placed to best communicate the meaning that the author intends?

   _____

   _____

6. Study the exercise until you are prepared for dictation.

Parse above the words:	PRO = pronoun	N = common noun	PN = proper noun	AV = action verb
	LV = linking verb	HV = helping verb	ADJ = adjective	ART = article
	ADV = adverb	PP = preposition	CON = conjunction	INT = interjection
	—inf— = infinitive	par = participle	ger = gerund	
Analyze below the words:	S = simple subject	P = simple predicate	DO = direct object	IO = indirect object
	PN = predicate nominative	PA = predicate adjective		
Identify clauses:	| independent clause |	< dependent clause >		

Lesson 92

(from Exercise 92, Robin Nests)

1. Read Exercise 92 in *Spelling Wisdom, Book 3.*

2. Parse and analyze the following sentence from the exercise. Watch for the infinitive.

> The conqueror's mate now proceeds to construct the nest in the chosen tree, while the other
>
> selects a spruce on the lawn at another side of the house.

3. Is that sentence simple, compound, complex, or compound-complex? Why?

   _____

   _____

4. What job is the dependent clause doing in that sentence from the exercise?

   _____

5. Tell whether the conjunction that begins the dependent clause in that sentence is coordinating or subordinating. (Use the lists on page 155 to help you if needed.)

   _____

6. How would the sentence's meaning change if one of the modifiers were moved to a different place? Read this rearrangement and note the different idea it communicates.

   > The conqueror's mate now proceeds to construct the nest, while the other selects a spruce on the lawn at another side of the house, in the chosen tree.

   _____

7. Study the exercise until you are prepared for dictation.

Parse above the words:	PRO = pronoun	N = common noun	PN = proper noun	AV = action verb
	LV = linking verb	HV = helping verb	ADJ = adjective	ART = article
	ADV = adverb	PP = preposition	CON = conjunction	INT = interjection
	—inf— = infinitive	par = participle	ger = gerund	
Analyze below the words:	S = simple subject	P = simple predicate	DO = direct object	IO = indirect object
	PN = predicate nominative	PA = predicate adjective		
Identify clauses:	| independent clause |	< dependent clause >		

Lesson 93
(from Exercise 93, Pliable Materials)

1. Read Exercise 93 in *Spelling Wisdom, Book 3*.

2. You have seen how dependent clauses can do the job of a modifier, acting as an adjective or an adverb in a sentence. In this exercise, you will see a dependent clause doing a different job; it is doing the job of a noun. Parse and analyze the following sentence to discover what role that noun clause is playing in the sentence.

   I found they were making sad havoc with some of my plants that had just been set out.

3. Tell all you have learned about dependent clauses, including what they are and what jobs they can do.

   _____

   _____

   _____

   _____

4. What have you learned about verbals? Explain the three kinds, the form of each, and what jobs they can do.

   _____

   _____

   _____

   _____

5. Study the exercise until you are prepared for dictation.

Parse above the words:	PRO = pronoun	N = common noun	PN = proper noun	AV = action verb
	LV = linking verb	HV = helping verb	ADJ = adjective	ART = article
	ADV = adverb	PP = preposition	CON = conjunction	INT = interjection
	—inf— = infinitive	par = participle	ger = gerund	
Analyze below the words:	S = simple subject	P = simple predicate	DO = direct object	IO = indirect object
	PN = predicate nominative	PA = predicate adjective		
Identify clauses:	| independent clause |	< dependent clause >		

Lesson 94

(from Exercise 94, Peace)

1. Read Exercise 94 in *Spelling Wisdom, Book 3.*

2. Remember that reading poetry slowly, clause by clause, and letting punctuation (rather than line breaks) dictate where you pause, will help you better understand what the poet was saying. Making sure that you know what each word means will also help. Define the words below, taking into consideration the context of the poem.

   • sentry _____

   • files _____

   • ranges _____

3. Now try to narrate the poem's main ideas. Put them into your own words.

   _____

   _____

   _____

4. Did you notice the personification used in the first six lines? Describe it.

   _____

   _____

5. What kind of rhyme scheme does this poem have?

   _____

6. Can you find the eye rhyme? What is it? _____

7. Describe the foot used in the lines of this poem. (Look back at Exercise 73 for help if you need it.)

   _____

8. A 3-foot line is called *trimeter.* (Notice the prefix *tri-*, as in *tricycle* or *triangle.*)
   A 4-foot line is called *tetrameter.*
   A 5-foot line is called *pentameter.*
   So this poem is written in iambic _____.

   The poem, "Daffodils," in Exercise 83, is written in iambic _____.

   "Breathes There the Man," in Exercise 73, is in iambic _____.

9. Study the poem until you are prepared for dictation.

Lesson 95
(from Exercise 95, Influence for Good)

1. Read Exercise 95 in *Spelling Wisdom, Book 3*.

2. Parse and analyze the following sentence from the exercise.

   No one could write such a history now.

3. What role is each of the following dependent clauses playing in the seventh sentence of the exercise?

   better than we can do now _____

   how great the apostle Paul was in the influence for good _____

   which he exerted _____

4. Explain what a parenthetical phrase is and the punctuation that goes with it.

   _____

   _____

5. Parenthetical phrases are nonessential to the sentence's meaning. It's the same with dependent clauses; many are not essential to understanding the sentence. But some dependent clauses are essential. Beside each dependent clause marked < > in the following sentences, write *E* or *NE* to signify whether it is essential or not essential to the sentence's meaning.

   I suppose we shall have such a history set before us < when we get to Heaven. >

   I hope you have kept me in remembrance and that I may always count on your friendship, < which is dear to me. >

   She skipped at last into the kitchen garden and saw Ben Weatherstaff digging and talking to his robin, < which was hopping about him. >

   But I am sure we all know in our hearts < that we have a great deal for which to be thankful. >

6. Look over those sentences and determine when a comma should be used to set off the dependent clause: when the clause is essential or not essential?

   _____

   Look for dependent clauses in future exercises to make sure of that guideline.

7. Study the exercise until you are prepared for dictation.

Parse above the words:	PRO = pronoun	N = common noun	PN = proper noun	AV = action verb
	LV = linking verb	HV = helping verb	ADJ = adjective	ART = article
	ADV = adverb	PP = preposition	CON = conjunction	INT = interjection
	—inf— = infinitive	par = participle	ger = gerund	
Analyze below the words:	S = simple subject	P = simple predicate	DO = direct object	IO = indirect object
	PN = predicate nominative	PA = predicate adjective		
Identify clauses:	| independent clause |	< dependent clause >		

Lesson 96
(from Exercise 96, First Night Stranded)

1. Read Exercise 96 in *Spelling Wisdom, Book 3.*

2. For each word below, find its synonym in the exercise.

   - protection _____
   - slumber _____
   - exhausted _____
   - work _____
   - rooster _____
   - welcomed _____
   - woke _____
   - dawn _____
   - pause _____
   - consultation _____
   - status _____
   - possibilities _____
   - determine _____
   - recent _____
   - marooned _____

3. Is the first sentence in the exercise simple, compound, complex, or compound-complex? Why?

   _____

   _____

4. Explain what job the dependent clause, "on which we were stranded," is doing in the last sentence.

   _____

5. Is that dependent clause essential or not essential for understanding the sentence's meaning?

   _____

   Another way to describe those two types of clauses is *restrictive* and *nonrestrictive*. A restrictive clause restricts the meaning of the term it modifies. In the sentence above, the dependent clause restricts exactly which *country* is being referred to. Is your comma guideline for clauses from Exercise 95 holding true, or does it need to be changed at all? Keep watching and observing until you're sure.

6. Study the exercise until you are prepared for dictation.

Lesson 97

(from Exercise 97, A Season of Prayer)

1. Read Exercise 97 in *Spelling Wisdom, Book 3*.

2. Parse and analyze the following sentence from the exercise.

   In the evening I withdrew and enjoyed a happy season in secret prayer.

   Analyzing Tip: Use the three-step process to help you analyze a sentence. See page 154 for details.

3. Now parse and analyze this excerpt from the exercise. Look for a gerund.

   I am persuaded they have been made a means of making me more humble and much more resigned.

4. What job is the gerund phrase doing in that sentence?

   _____

5. Explain why each comma is in the final sentence of the exercise. (Look at the Comma Guidelines on page 153 for help if you need it.)
   - Oh, _____
   - come, _____
   - Jesus, _____

6. Study the exercise until you are prepared for dictation.

Parse above the words:	PRO = pronoun	N = common noun	PN = proper noun	AV = action verb
	LV = linking verb	HV = helping verb	ADJ = adjective	ART = article
	ADV = adverb	PP = preposition	CON = conjunction	INT = interjection
	—inf— = infinitive	par = participle	ger = gerund	
Analyze below the words:	S = simple subject	P = simple predicate	DO = direct object	IO = indirect object
	PN = predicate nominative	PA = predicate adjective		
Identify clauses:	| independent clause |	< dependent clause >		

Lesson 98

(from Exercise 98, Barrels of Honey)

1. Read Exercise 98 in *Spelling Wisdom, Book 3*.

2. Parse and analyze the following sentence from the exercise.

> **Whenever one received a present, the other two were each given one of equal value.**

3. What role is the dependent clause playing in that sentence? _____

4. Notice how that dependent clause acts like an introductory thought that sets the stage for the independent clause that follows. Introductory phrases can do that too. The following sentences from previous exercises contain introductory phrases and clauses. Underline each introductory phrase and mark each introductory dependent clause with < >. Also look for a pattern in the punctuation used with those introductory groups of words, whether phrases or dependent clauses.

> Until this artist's time, people had been used only to great canvases and had grown to look for fine work only in much space.

> With all the eagerness which such a transition gives, Emma resolved to be out of doors as soon as possible.

> Talking to himself, he said, "In school today I'll learn to read."

> When the sun peeped into the girls' room early next morning to promise them a fine day, he saw a comical sight.

> Record on page 153 what you discovered about punctuation for introductory phrases and dependent clauses that set the stage.

5. Parse and analyze the following sentence from the exercise. The dependent clause will be acting as a noun; watch for it. And also watch for a gerund.

> **Can you show how they succeeded in making a correct division of the property?**

6. Can you solve the mathematical puzzle presented in the exercise?

_____

7. Study the exercise until you are prepared for dictation.

Parse above the words:	PRO = pronoun	N = common noun	PN = proper noun	AV = action verb
	LV = linking verb	HV = helping verb	ADJ = adjective	ART = article
	ADV = adverb	PP = preposition	CON = conjunction	INT = interjection
	—inf— = infinitive	par = participle	ger = gerund	
Analyze below the words:	S = simple subject	P = simple predicate	DO = direct object	IO = indirect object
	PN = predicate nominative	PA = predicate adjective		
Identify clauses:	| independent clause |	< dependent clause >		

Lesson 99
(from Exercise 99, The Footprint)

1. Read Exercise 99 in *Spelling Wisdom, Book 3*.

2. Detail the differences between the three verbals.

Verbal	Form	Job
Gerund	_____	_____
Participle	_____	_____
Infinitive	_____	_____
	_____	_____

3. Parse and analyze the following sentence from the exercise. You should find two nonrestrictive (nonessential) dependent clauses and an introductory participial phrase.

   It happened one day about noon, going towards my boat, I was exceedingly surprised with the

   print of a man's naked foot on the shore, which was very plain to be seen on the sand.

   Analyzing Tip: *Use the three-step process to help you analyze a sentence. See page 154 for details.*

4. Explain why each comma is in that sentence.
   - noon, _____
   - boat, _____
   - shore, _____

5. Summarize what you have discovered about comma usage with essential (restrictive) and nonessential (nonrestrictive) words, phrases, and clauses in a sentence. Write your summary as a new guideline on page 153.

6. Study the exercise until you are prepared for dictation.

Parse above the words:	PRO = pronoun	N = common noun	PN = proper noun	AV = action verb
	LV = linking verb	HV = helping verb	ADJ = adjective	ART = article
	ADV = adverb	PP = preposition	CON = conjunction	INT = interjection
	—inf— = infinitive	par = participle	ger = gerund	
Analyze below the words:	S = simple subject	P = simple predicate	DO = direct object	IO = indirect object
	PN = predicate nominative	PA = predicate adjective		
Identify clauses:	| independent clause |	< dependent clause >		

Lesson 100
(from Exercise 100, Poor Richard's Almanac)

1. Read Exercise 100 in *Spelling Wisdom, Book 3.*

2. Explain why each punctuation mark is in the first two sentences of the exercise.

    • Saunders; _____

    • twenty-five _____

    • years, _____

    • Richard's _____

    • Almanac. _____

    • useful, _____

    • it, _____

    • thousand. _____

3. Define these words as they are used in the context of the exercise. Use a dictionary for help.

    • remarkable _____

    • proverbial _____

    • inculcated _____

    • industry _____

    • frugality _____

    • procuring _____

    • virtue _____

4. Explain the proverb comparison Benjamin Franklin made in the final sentence. Do you agree with it? Why?

    _____

    _____

    _____

    _____

    _____

5. Study the exercise until you are prepared for dictation.

Lesson 101

(from Exercise 101, Condolences)

1. Read Exercise 101 in *Spelling Wisdom, Book 3.*

2. Determine whether each of the following phrases from the exercise is a prepositional phrase or an infinitive phrase.

   to all _____

   to the young _____

   to ever expect it _____

   to afford some alleviation _____

   to be happy again _____

   To know this _____

   to your afflicted mother _____

3. Parse and analyze the following sentence from the exercise. Watch for an infinitive phrase doing the work of a noun.

   The older have learned to ever expect it.

4. The following words from the exercise have suffixes and prefixes. Detail each one's root word and how its prefix or suffix has changed its meaning or part of speech.

   unawares

   Root: _____

   Change: _____

   alleviation

   Root: _____

   Change: _____

   holier

   Root: _____

   Change: _____

5. Study the exercise until you are prepared for dictation.

Parse above the words:	PRO = pronoun	N = common noun	PN = proper noun	AV = action verb
	LV = linking verb	HV = helping verb	ADJ = adjective	ART = article
	ADV = adverb	PP = preposition	CON = conjunction	INT = interjection
	—inf— = infinitive	par = participle	ger = gerund	
Analyze below the words:	S = simple subject	P = simple predicate	DO = direct object	IO = indirect object
	PN = predicate nominative	PA = predicate adjective		
Identify clauses:	| independent clause |	< dependent clause >		

Lesson 102

(from Exercise 102, Stanley's Courage)

1. Read Exercise 102 in *Spelling Wisdom, Book 3*.

2. Why is there a comma after "Sitting in our quiet American homes,"? (Look back at Lesson 98 if you need a reminder.)

_____

3. Why are there commas between "civilization, peace, and comfort"?

_____

4. Explain why there is a colon after "One thing was in Stanley's favor."

_____

5. What job are the dashes doing in the final paragraph of the exercise?

_____

6. Why are the commas between the dashes?

_____

7. Parse and analyze the following excerpt from the exercise.

it was necessary for him to exercise all his ingenuity and show all his courage in overcoming

difficulties and pushing forward in his great undertaking.

Analyzing Tip: Use the three-step process to help you analyze a sentence. See page 154 for details.

8. Study the exercise until you are prepared for dictation.

Parse above the words:	PRO = pronoun LV = linking verb ADV = adverb —inf— = infinitive	N = common noun HV = helping verb PP = preposition par = participle	PN = proper noun ADJ = adjective CON = conjunction ger = gerund	AV = action verb ART = article INT = interjection
Analyze below the words:	S = simple subject PN = predicate nominative	P = simple predicate PA = predicate adjective	DO = direct object	IO = indirect object
Identify clauses:	| independent clause |	< dependent clause >		

Lesson 103

(from Exercise 103, Salvaging Iron)

1. Read Exercise 103 in *Spelling Wisdom, Book 3.*

2. Since a participle acts as a modifier, you should always be able to find the word in the sentence that it modifies. In the following excerpts from the exercise, underline each participial phrase and circle the word that it modifies.

   having plundered the ship of what was portable and fit to hand out, I began with the cables

   Cutting the great cable into pieces such as I could move, I got two cables and a hawser on shore

3. Do the same with this excerpt from Exercise 17.

   There was another vessel before them, toiling and laboring in the howling storm

    Writing Point: *Make sure your sentences give the word that any participle is modifying. A participle without a word to modify is called a* dangling participle.

4. What does *fain* mean, as used in the next to last sentence of Exercise 103? Look up its definition based on the context of the sentence, then put that clause into your own words.

   _____

   _____

   _____

   _____

5. Study the exercise until you are prepared for dictation.

Lesson 104
(from Exercise 104, Home-Thoughts from Abroad)

1. Read Exercise 104 in *Spelling Wisdom, Book 3.*

2. What does the title tell you about this poem's setting?

3. How would you describe the tone of Browning's words?

4. What is the rhyme scheme he used? (Be sure to analyze both stanzas.)

5. Explain what *iambic trimeter, iambic tetrameter,* and *iambic pentameter* mean.

6. Would you say this poem fits any of those descriptions? Why do you suppose that is?

7. What would you say the poet missed most about England?

8. Study the poem until you are prepared for dictation.

Lesson 105

(from Exercise 105, The Bell of Justice)

1. Read Exercise 105 in *Spelling Wisdom, Book 3*.

2. Find the four times in the exercise that the writer mentions the horse. Record the four descriptions that the writer used to refer to it.

   _____

   _____

3. Why do you suppose the author used those different word combinations when referring to the same thing?

   _____

4. Explain why each of the punctuation marks is in the excerpt below.

   "What!" said he, "this faithful creature has toiled all its life for you

   • "What _____

   • What! _____

   • What!" _____

   • he, _____

   • "this _____

5. Why is *this* not capitalized in the dialogue written above?

   _____

   _____

6. Parse and analyze the following sentence from the exercise.

   This bell the king called the "Bell of Justice."

7. Study the exercise until you are prepared for dictation.

Parse above the words:	PRO = pronoun	N = common noun	PN = proper noun	AV = action verb
	LV = linking verb	HV = helping verb	ADJ = adjective	ART = article
	ADV = adverb	PP = preposition	CON = conjunction	INT = interjection
	—inf— = infinitive	par = participle	ger = gerund	
Analyze below the words:	S = simple subject	P = simple predicate	DO = direct object	IO = indirect object
	PN = predicate nominative	PA = predicate adjective		
Identify clauses:	| independent clause |	< dependent clause >		

Lesson 106

(from Exercise 106, Nature Study)

1. Read Exercise 106 in *Spelling Wisdom, Book 3.*

2. Parse and analyze the following clause from the exercise.

   He would lie on the grass

3. People often get *lie* and *lay* mixed up. *Lie* means "to recline"; *lay* means "to place." One easy way to know which word to use is to determine whether that verb has an object. "To recline" does not require an object, but if you're going "to place" something somewhere, you usually tell what *something* was placed—an object—as "I will lay *the book* on the shelf."

   Which word would be correct to use in these lines from "Daffodils"?

   For oft when on my couch I _____

   In vacant or in pensive mood,

4. Notice all of the possessive words listed in the last sentence of Exercise 106. Which ones are spelled with *'s* and which with *s'*? Why? What is the difference?

   _____

   _____

   _____

5. Study the exercise until you are prepared for dictation.

Parse above the words:	PRO = pronoun	N = common noun	PN = proper noun	AV = action verb
	LV = linking verb	HV = helping verb	ADJ = adjective	ART = article
	ADV = adverb	PP = preposition	CON = conjunction	INT = interjection
	—inf— = infinitive	par = participle	ger = gerund	
Analyze below the words:	S = simple subject	P = simple predicate	DO = direct object	IO = indirect object
	PN = predicate nominative	PA = predicate adjective		
Identify clauses:	| independent clause |	< dependent clause >		

Lesson 107

(from Exercise 107, The Most Important Day)

1. Read Exercise 107 in *Spelling Wisdom, Book 3*.

2. In the second paragraph, why is the apostrophe before the *s* in *mother's*?

   _____

3. Parse and analyze the following sentence from the exercise. Look for a compound predicate verb.

   The afternoon sun penetrated the mass of honeysuckle that covered the porch, and fell on my

   upturned face.

4. Usually you should never separate the subject and predicate verb with a comma. Why do you suppose an exception was made in the above sentence from the exercise?

   _____

   _____

   Record a comma guideline on page 153 to remind you of this exception.

   Writing Point: *Be familiar with the set guidelines for comma usage in your writing, but know that you can always insert a comma to clarify your meaning as needed.*

5. Define the following words from the last sentence of the exercise, then rewrite the sentence in your own words.

   • preyed _____

   • languor _____

   • succeeded _____

   • passionate _____

   _____

6. Study the exercise until you are prepared for dictation.

Parse above the words:	PRO = pronoun	N = common noun	PN = proper noun	AV = action verb
	LV = linking verb	HV = helping verb	ADJ = adjective	ART = article
	ADV = adverb	PP = preposition	CON = conjunction	INT = interjection
	—inf— = infinitive	par = participle	ger = gerund	
Analyze below the words:	S = simple subject	P = simple predicate	DO = direct object	IO = indirect object
	PN = predicate nominative	PA = predicate adjective		
Identify clauses:	| independent clause |	< dependent clause >		

Lesson 108
(from Exercise 108, Two Houses)

1. Read Exercise 108 in *Spelling Wisdom, Book 3*.

2. Explain the difference between *lay* and *lie*. (Look back at Lesson 106 for help if you need it.)

    _____

    _____

3. Now look near the end of Exercise 108 and you will see the past tense of *lie* used in a clause. Write the word where it belongs in the chart below.

	Present	Past	Past Participle
Lie (to recline)	*Lie*	_____	*Lain*
Lay (to place)	*Lay*	*Laid*	*Laid*

4. How do you know the author meant "to recline" in that clause?

    _____

    _____

5. What if the author had added an object and written "and here I _____ my head at night"? Which word should be used in that case? (Remember, the author was writing in past tense.)

    _____

    Writing Point: It will be helpful to memorize the chart above, so you can use the correct words to convey your exact meaning in your writing.

6. Which word from the chart should be used in the sentence below? Try to determine the correct word for yourself, then look back at Exercise 74 to see if you chose the right one.

    There was a delightful freshness in the air the other morning, and all over the low places _____ the first frost of the season.

7. Study the exercise until you are prepared for dictation.

Lesson 109

(from Exercise 109, Plans for Colin)

1. Read Exercise 109 in *Spelling Wisdom, Book 3*.

2. Parse and analyze the following sentence from the exercise. The dependent clause is doing the job of a noun.

   No one must ever suspect that they had a secret.

   🔍 ***Analyzing Tip:*** *Use the three-step process to help you analyze a sentence. See page 154 for details.*

3. Now parse and analyze the sentence below.

   They would turn into the shrubbery walks and lose themselves until they came to the long walls.

4. Do you remember the difference between *lose* and *loose*? For each clause below, determine which of the two words should be used. Look back at the noted exercises to check your work.

   Although a man may _____ a sense of his own importance when he is a mere unit among a busy throng . . . (Exercise 24)

   Now, as the bicycle cost the salesman £11, how much money did he _____ altogether? (Exercise 47)

   . . . a waistcoat, and breeches open at the knees, and both _____ , for they were rather wanting to keep me cool than to keep me warm. (Exercise 60)

5. Study the exercise until you are prepared for dictation.

Parse above the words:	PRO = pronoun	N = common noun	PN = proper noun	AV = action verb
	LV = linking verb	HV = helping verb	ADJ = adjective	ART = article
	ADV = adverb	PP = preposition	CON = conjunction	INT = interjection
	—inf— = infinitive	par = participle	ger = gerund	
Analyze below the words:	S = simple subject	P = simple predicate	DO = direct object	IO = indirect object
	PN = predicate nominative	PA = predicate adjective		
Identify clauses:	| independent clause |	< dependent clause >		

Lesson 110
(from Exercise 110, Mercy on a Mouse)

1. Read Exercise 110 in *Spelling Wisdom, Book 3*.

2. Parse and analyze the following sentence from the exercise.

   Alexander Wilson, the great lover and student of birds, relates a touching experience with a

   mouse.

3. Find the appositive in that sentence. Record the appositive and describe the punctuation connected to it. (Look back at Lesson 86 if you need help.)

   _____

   _____

4. Look for the appositive in Exercise 107 (first paragraph) and Exercise 109 (second paragraph) and see if the punctuation is similar. Record your findings as the final new comma guideline on page 153.

5. Explain why the colon is used in the second sentence of Exercise 110.

   _____

   _____

6. How do you know the rest of the exercise is one long quotation? (Hint: Look at the beginnings and endings of each paragraph.)

   _____

   _____

7. Study the exercise until you are prepared for dictation.

Parse above the words:	PRO = pronoun	N = common noun	PN = proper noun	AV = action verb
	LV = linking verb	HV = helping verb	ADJ = adjective	ART = article
	ADV = adverb	PP = preposition	CON = conjunction	INT = interjection
	—inf— = infinitive	par = participle	ger = gerund	
Analyze below the words:	S = simple subject	P = simple predicate	DO = direct object	IO = indirect object
	PN = predicate nominative	PA = predicate adjective		
Identify clauses:	| independent clause |	< dependent clause >		

Lesson 111

(from Exercise 111, Holman Hunt)

1. Read Exercise 111 in *Spelling Wisdom, Book 3.*

2. Parse and analyze the following excerpt from the exercise. Watch for the gerund.

    The designing of calicoes can hardly be called art

3. Now parse and analyze the sentence below. It has a gerund too.

    He found in his new place another clerk who cared for art, and this sympathy encouraged him

    to fix his mind upon painting more than ever.

4. The adjective clause, "who cared for art," modifies which noun? _____

5. Mark the adjective or adverb clauses < > in the sentences below. Beside each sentence write *R* if the clause is restrictive or *NR* if it is nonrestrictive.

    ____ **Men who had only known the quiet thinker and logician of Baker Street would have failed to recognize him.**

    ____ **Gentlemen, which means boys, be courteous to the old maids**

    ____ **You must have started early, and yet you had a good drive in a dog-cart along heavy roads before you reached the station.**

    ____ **Now the males, which appear to be jealous of one another, have many fierce battles.**

6. Study the exercise until you are prepared for dictation.

Parse above the words:	PRO = pronoun	N = common noun	PN = proper noun	AV = action verb
	LV = linking verb	HV = helping verb	ADJ = adjective	ART = article
	ADV = adverb	PP = preposition	CON = conjunction	INT = interjection
	—inf— = infinitive	par = participle	ger = gerund	
Analyze below the words:	S = simple subject	P = simple predicate	DO = direct object	IO = indirect object
	PN = predicate nominative	PA = predicate adjective		
Identify clauses:	| independent clause |	< dependent clause >		

Lesson 112
(from Exercise 112, The Title Deed)

1. Read Exercise 112 in *Spelling Wisdom, Book 3.*

2. Parse and analyze the following sentence from the exercise. Look for a participle.

   The property described in it could never become ours unless the queen's signature and seal were

   added to it.

3. What job is the participial phrase "described in it" doing?

   _____

4. Why is there no comma to set off that phrase from the rest of the sentence?

   _____

5. What kind of sentence is it: simple, compound, complex, or compound-complex?

   _____

6. Underline the two prepositional phrases in the excerpt below.

   It would be stated here how many acres of land were connected with it

7. One of those prepositional phrases comes between a subject and its verb. Which one is it?

   _____

   It is important to make sure the subject and verb agree in number, especially when other words come between them. If a person wasn't paying attention, he might think that the singular noun *land* was the subject and write, "how many acres of land *was* connected with it." But the true subject is the plural noun *acres* so, "how many acres . . . *were* connected" is correct. Don't be fooled by words, phrases, or clauses sitting between the subject and verb. Make sure they agree in number.

8. Study the exercise until you are prepared for dictation.

Parse above the words:	PRO = pronoun	N = common noun	PN = proper noun	AV = action verb
	LV = linking verb	HV = helping verb	ADJ = adjective	ART = article
	ADV = adverb	PP = preposition	CON = conjunction	INT = interjection
	—inf— = infinitive	par = participle	ger = gerund	
Analyze below the words:	S = simple subject	P = simple predicate	DO = direct object	IO = indirect object
	PN = predicate nominative	PA = predicate adjective		
Identify clauses:	| independent clause |	< dependent clause >		

Lesson 113

(from Exercise 113, The Rich Treasure)

1. Read Exercise 113 in *Spelling Wisdom, Book 3.*

2. In what tense is the exercise written: present tense or past tense? _____

3. Complete the chart below that details how to use *lay* and *lie.* Circle the word on the chart that is used in the third sentence of the exercise. (Keep in mind the tense in which it is written.)

	Present	Past	Past Participle
Lie (to _____ *)*	_____	_____	*Lain*
Lay (to _____ *)*	_____	*Laid*	*Laid*

4. In the following sentence from the exercise, mark the two subjects and their corresponding predicate verbs.

   He never had supposed for a moment that so large a sum as a hundred dollars was to be found

   in actual money in any one's possession.

5. Underline the phrase that is between the second subject and its verb. Explain what you learned in Lesson 112 about not being fooled by words, phrases, and clauses that come between subjects and verbs.

   _____

   _____

   _____

6. Explain why each comma is in the final sentence of the exercise.

   _____

   _____

   _____

   _____

7. Study the exercise until you are prepared for dictation.

Lesson 114
(from Exercise 114, Common Sense)

1. Read Exercise 114 in *Spelling Wisdom, Book 3*.

2. Describe the comparison and contrast that James Thomas Fields presented in the poem.

   _____

   _____

   _____

   _____

   _____

   _____

3. Put the poet's conclusion in your own words. Do you agree with him? Explain.

   _____

   _____

   _____

   _____

4. The entire poem is a personification. Explain what that means and how the poem fits that description.

   _____

   _____

   _____

5. Now analyze the poem's structure.
   - Number of stanzas: _____
   - Lines per stanza: _____
   - Rhyme scheme: _____
   - Syllables per line: _____ _____
   - Foot (give the official name): _____
   - Foot per line (give the official name): _____

6. Study the poem until you are prepared for dictation.

Lesson 115
(from Exercise 115, The Lion's Voice)

1. Read Exercise 115 in *Spelling Wisdom, Book 3.*

2. Use a dictionary to help you define each of the following words, taking into consideration the context of the exercise.

    • peculiarly _____

    • striking _____

    • audible _____

    • solemn _____

    • succession _____

    • concert _____

    • catch _____

    • stags _____

    • intensely _____

    • defiance _____

    • vie _____

3. Several of those words contain a suffix that changes the word to a different part of speech. Complete the chart below as you look more closely at those words.

Word	Part of Speech	Root Word	Part of Speech
Peculiarly	_____	*Peculiar*	_____
Striking	_____	*Strike*	_____
Succession	_____	*Succeed*	_____
Intensely	_____	*Intense*	_____
Defiance	_____	*Defy*	_____

4. Find the simile in the second paragraph. What is being compared?

    _____

    _____

5. Study the exercise until you are prepared for dictation.

Lesson 116

(from Exercise 116, The Babies' Names)

1. Read Exercise 116 in *Spelling Wisdom, Book 3.*

2. Parse and analyze the following sentence from the exercise.

   When an infant is born in a family, it is generally the occasion of great interest.

3. What job is the dependent clause performing? _____

4. Explain why there is a comma after that clause.

   _____

5. In the sentence below, explain why there is a comma after dear and no comma after Ireland.

   I had a dear, good minister from Ireland staying at my house not long ago.

   _____

   _____

6. Why did the minister's quotation start with, "Sure and"? What clue can you find earlier in the exercise?

   _____

7. Why is the possessive word in the title of the exercise spelled *Babies'* rather than *Baby's*? Explain the difference between those two words.

   _____

   _____

   _____

   _____

8. Study the exercise until you are prepared for dictation.

Parse above the words:	PRO = pronoun	N = common noun	PN = proper noun	AV = action verb
	LV = linking verb	HV = helping verb	ADJ = adjective	ART = article
	ADV = adverb	PP = preposition	CON = conjunction	INT = interjection
	—inf— = infinitive	par = participle	ger = gerund	
Analyze below the words:	S = simple subject	P = simple predicate	DO = direct object	IO = indirect object
	PN = predicate nominative	PA = predicate adjective		
Identify clauses:	| independent clause |	< dependent clause >		

Lesson 117

(from Exercise 117, A Night in Prison)

1. Read Exercise 117 in *Spelling Wisdom, Book 3.*

2. Tell what the following phrase from the first sentence of the exercise is called and explain the job it does: "the father of the queens Elizabeth and Mary."

   _____

   _____

3. Parse and analyze the following sentence from the exercise.

   But he would not tell them who he was.

4. Explain what job the clause "who he was" is doing in that sentence. _____

5. In the following sentence from the exercise, explain why there is a comma after "on getting back to his palace" and no comma before "where he had spent the night."

   On getting back to his palace, one of the first things he did was to send a sum of money to the keeper of the prison where he had spent the night.

   _____

   _____

   _____

   _____

6. In the exercise, find

   • an antonym for *recognized* _____

   • a synonym for *liberated* _____

   • a homonym for *mourning* _____

7. Study the exercise until you are prepared for dictation.

Parse above the words:	PRO = pronoun	N = common noun	PN = proper noun	AV = action verb
	LV = linking verb	HV = helping verb	ADJ = adjective	ART = article
	ADV = adverb	PP = preposition	CON = conjunction	INT = interjection
	—inf— = infinitive	par = participle	ger = gerund	
Analyze below the words:	S = simple subject	P = simple predicate	DO = direct object	IO = indirect object
	PN = predicate nominative	PA = predicate adjective		
Identify clauses:	| independent clause |	< dependent clause >		

Lesson 118

(from Exercise 118, Dependent on God)

1. Read Exercise 118 in *Spelling Wisdom, Book 3*.

2. For each word from the exercise listed below, write the root form and tell what each prefix or suffix has changed about it, either in meaning or part of speech. The first one is done for you.

helplessness
Root: *help*

less—changed meaning to opposite ("help" to "helpless")

ness—changed part of speech from adjective ("helpless") to noun ("helplessness")

inability
Root: _____

_____

_____

dependent
Root: _____

_____

assistance
Root: _____

_____

insufficiency
Root: _____

_____

_____

considerable
Root: _____

_____

enabled
Root: _____

_____

_____

3. Study the exercise until you are prepared for dictation.

Lesson 119

(from Exercise 119, The Angel in the Stone)

1. Read Exercise 119 in *Spelling Wisdom, Book 3*.

2. Find the participial phrases that modify the following nouns and pronoun from the exercise.

Nouns	Participial Phrases
He loved to see beautiful **figures**	_____
he saw a **block** *of marble*	_____
he saw a **block** *of marble*	_____
he *threw off his coat and went to work*	_____

3. Explain the difference between *lay* and *lie*.

_____

_____

4. Complete the chart below that details how to use *lay* and *lie*. Circle the word on the chart that is used in the fourth sentence of the exercise. Notice how the word's spelling changes with the addition of the suffix *ing*.

	Present	Past	Past Participle
Lie (to _____)	_____	_____	*Lain*
Lay (to _____)	_____	*Laid*	*Laid*

5. Which word should be used in the sentence below (with an *-ing* suffix)? Write the correct word in the blank, then look back at Exercise 48 to check your answer.

   A lens and a forceps _____ **upon the seat of the chair suggested that the hat had been suspended in this manner for the purpose of examination.**

6. Study the exercise until you are prepared for dictation.

Lesson 120
(from Exercise 120, Learning Outdoors)

1. Read Exercise 120 in *Spelling Wisdom, Book 3*.

2. Parse and analyze the following sentence from the exercise. Look for the participle.

   We read and studied out of doors, preferring the sunlit woods to the house.

3. Explain why the comma is used in that sentence.

   _____

   _____

4. What noun or pronoun in the sentence does the participial phrase modify? _____

5. What kind of sentence is it: simple, compound, complex, or compound-complex? Explain your answer.

   _____

6. Read through the exercise again and note which of the five senses are employed in the descriptions.

   _____

7. Consider who wrote the passage and what you know about that author. Does that alter the mental picture you have of the use of those senses? How?

   _____

   _____

   Writing Point: *It is amazing how vivid the descriptions are in the exercise. Such descriptive wording helps the reader easily imagine the scene. Keep in mind that painting a vivid word picture of a setting usually includes more than one sense—not just what is seen.*

8. Study the exercise until you are prepared for dictation.

Parse above the words:	PRO = pronoun	N = common noun	PN = proper noun	AV = action verb
	LV = linking verb	HV = helping verb	ADJ = adjective	ART = article
	ADV = adverb	PP = preposition	CON = conjunction	INT = interjection
	—inf— = infinitive	par = participle	ger = gerund	
Analyze below the words:	S = simple subject	P = simple predicate	DO = direct object	IO = indirect object
	PN = predicate nominative	PA = predicate adjective		
Identify clauses:	| independent clause |	< dependent clause >		

Lesson 121
(from Exercise 121, Native Rabbit)

1. Read Exercise 121 in *Spelling Wisdom, Book 3*.

2. Explain why the two commas are in the first sentence.

    • office, _____

    • station, _____

3. Explain why each mark of punctuation is in the fifth sentence of the exercise.

    • "Yes _____

    • Yes, _____

    • lord, _____

    • lord," _____

    • replied, _____

    • "rabbit _____

    • jungles. _____

    • jungles." _____

4. Why is "rabbit" not capitalized?

    _____

    _____

5. The rest of the exercise has no dialogue tags that tell who is speaking. How do you know who spoke each statement?

    _____

    _____

Writing Point: A dialogue without dialogue tags moves faster than one with tags. However, be careful that you don't leave your reader confused about who is speaking. Insert enough dialogue tags and conversational clues to help readers stay on track.

6. Jules Verne's choice of two words influences the reader's opinion about one of the characters in that dialogue: "rogue boldly." What was the author trying to communicate about the landlord by using that noun and that adverb?

    _____

    _____

7. Study the exercise until you are prepared for dictation.

Lesson 122
(from Exercise 122, Athletic Sports)

1. Read Exercise 122 in *Spelling Wisdom, Book 3.*

2. Explain why each of these marks of punctuation is used in the final sentence of the exercise.

   - Mars; _____

   - field; _____

   - courts; _____

   - bull, _____

   - arrive, _____

   - heels. _____

3. Why do you suppose the author chose to use *fringed* in this clause: "croquet mallets clicked under the elms that fringed the field." What other words could have been used? Explain which would be the best choice and why.

   _____

   _____

   _____

4. Alphabetize the following list of book titles from previous exercises. (Look back at Lesson 25 if you need to review how to alphabetize titles with articles correctly.)

   The Story of My Life   _____

   The Adventures of Sherlock Holmes   _____

   The Secret Garden   _____

   The Swiss Family Robinson   _____

   The Autobiography of Benjamin Franklin   _____

   The Adventures of Tom Sawyer   _____

5. Study the exercise until you are prepared for dictation.

Lesson 123
(from Exercise 123, An Old Woman of the Roads)

1. Read Exercise 123 in *Spelling Wisdom, Book 3.*

2. Whose point of view is expressed in the words of the poem? How can you tell?

   _____

   _____

3. Describe the tone of the poem. What emotions come through and what words contribute to that tone?

   _____

   _____

   _____

4. Define the terms below in order to have a clearer mental picture of the poem. As always, take into consideration the context.

   • turf _____

   • delph _____

   • store _____

   • bog _____

5. Now analyze the poem's structure.

   • Number of stanzas: _____

   • Lines per stanza: _____

   • Rhyme scheme: _____

   • Syllables per line (most lines): _____

   • Foot (give the official name): _____

   • Foot per line (give the official name): _____

6. Study the poem until you are prepared for dictation.

Lesson 124
(from Exercise 124, Winter Near the Wild Wood)

1. Read Exercise 124 in *Spelling Wisdom, Book 3.*

2. Parse and analyze the following sentence from the exercise.

   It was a cold still afternoon with a hard steely sky overhead when he slipped out of the warm

   parlor into the open air.

3. Explain what job the dependent clause is doing. _____

4. What kind of sentence is that: simple, compound, complex, or compound-complex? Explain your answer.

   _____

   _____

5. What kind of picture was the author trying to paint with the choice of the adjectives *hard* and *steely*?

   _____

   _____

6. Explain the ideas that are communicated by the three carefully-chosen adjectives in the following sentence.

   It was pitiful in a way, and yet cheering—even exhilarating.

   _____

   _____

   _____

   ✎ **Writing Point:** *Kenneth Grahame was a master of word choice. Read his works to enjoy and learn!*

7. Study the exercise until you are prepared for dictation.

Parse above the words:	PRO = pronoun	N = common noun	PN = proper noun	AV = action verb
	LV = linking verb	HV = helping verb	ADJ = adjective	ART = article
	ADV = adverb	PP = preposition	CON = conjunction	INT = interjection
	—inf— = infinitive	par = participle	ger = gerund	
Analyze below the words:	S = simple subject	P = simple predicate	DO = direct object	IO = indirect object
	PN = predicate nominative	PA = predicate adjective		
Identify clauses:	| independent clause |	< dependent clause >		

Lesson 125
(from Exercise 125, Swimming for Father)

1. Read Exercise 125 in *Spelling Wisdom, Book 3*.

2. Parse and analyze the following sentence from the exercise.

    At dawn he saw, not far away from him, a long stretch of sand.

3. Explain why the two commas are in that sentence.

    _____   _____

    _____

4. How could you rearrange that sentence so it would not need the commas?

    _____

    _____

5. Which arrangement do you think is strongest? Why?

    _____

    _____

6. Explain why the comma is in the following sentence.

    Pinocchio tried his best to get there, but he couldn't.

    _____

7. Study the exercise until you are prepared for dictation.

Parse above the words:	PRO = pronoun	N = common noun	PN = proper noun	AV = action verb
	LV = linking verb	HV = helping verb	ADJ = adjective	ART = article
	ADV = adverb	PP = preposition	CON = conjunction	INT = interjection
	—inf— = infinitive	par = participle	ger = gerund	
Analyze below the words:	S = simple subject	P = simple predicate	DO = direct object	IO = indirect object
	PN = predicate nominative	PA = predicate adjective		
Identify clauses:	| independent clause |	< dependent clause >		

Lesson 126

(from Exercise 126, After Ten Years)

1. Read Exercise 126 in *Spelling Wisdom, Book 3.*

2. Complete the chart below that details how to use *lay* and *lie.* Circle the word on the chart that is used in the second sentence of the exercise.

	Present	Past	Past Participle
Lie (to _____)	_____	_____	*Lain*
Lay (to _____)	_____	_____	*Laid*

3. Detail the root word, suffix, and prefix of *imperceptibly.* Explain how each suffix and prefix changes the word, either in meaning or part of speech.

   Root: _____

   _____

   _____

4. Explain why each mark of punctuation is in the second paragraph of the exercise.

   • year; _____

   • chapter; _____

   • steadily, _____

   • imperceptibly, _____

   • away. _____

5. Why do you suppose Johann Wyss listed the adverbs first in the final clause of that paragraph? What mood does that word order convey in that sentence?

   _____

   _____

   _____

   Writing Point: Word order can be just as important as word choice in your writing.

6. Study the exercise until you are prepared for dictation.

Lesson 127

(from Exercise 127, The Officer Helps)

1. Read Exercise 127 in *Spelling Wisdom, Book 3.*

2. Identify the subject and predicate verb of the independent clause in the first sentence of the exercise.

   _____

3. What are the two prepositional phrases that come between that subject and verb?

   _____

4. Explain what it means to make the subject and the verb agree in number.

   _____

   _____

5. How can interrupting prepositional phrases sometimes confuse a writer into using the wrong verb and ending up with a subject and verb that don't agree? Give an example, using the phrasing from the sentence you identified above.

   _____

   _____

   _____

6. Explain why each comma is in that first sentence of the exercise.

   • Revolution, _____

   • works, _____

7. Parse and analyze the following sentence from the exercise.

   He took out his handkerchief and wiped his brow.

8. Study the exercise until you are prepared for dictation.

Parse above the words:	PRO = pronoun	N = common noun	PN = proper noun	AV = action verb
	LV = linking verb	HV = helping verb	ADJ = adjective	ART = article
	ADV = adverb	PP = preposition	CON = conjunction	INT = interjection
	—inf— = infinitive	par = participle	ger = gerund	
Analyze below the words:	S = simple subject	P = simple predicate	DO = direct object	IO = indirect object
	PN = predicate nominative	PA = predicate adjective		
Identify clauses:	| independent clause |	< dependent clause >		

Lesson 128
(from Exercise 128, God Does All Things Well)

1. Read Exercise 128 in *Spelling Wisdom, Book 3*.

2. Parse and analyze the following sentence from the exercise.

    The socket for each of your eyes and each of my eyes just fits it.

    Analyzing Tip: Use the three-step process to help you analyze a sentence. See page 154 for details.

3. What other words could an inattentive writer mistake for the subject and thus get the subject and verb agreement wrong?

    _____

    _____

4. In two places in the exercise, you will find a word that renames the preceding word. Look for those two instances and complete them below.

    he knew how large to make the basin _____

    each eye has a little hole _____

5. How are those terms similar to an appositive?

    _____

    _____

6. How are they different from an appositive?

    _____

7. Study the exercise until you are prepared for dictation.

Parse above the words:	PRO = pronoun	N = common noun	PN = proper noun	AV = action verb
	LV = linking verb	HV = helping verb	ADJ = adjective	ART = article
	ADV = adverb	PP = preposition	CON = conjunction	INT = interjection
	—inf— = infinitive	par = participle	ger = gerund	
Analyze below the words:	S = simple subject	P = simple predicate	DO = direct object	IO = indirect object
	PN = predicate nominative	PA = predicate adjective		
Identify clauses:	| independent clause |	< dependent clause >		

Lesson 129
(from Exercise 129, The Banquet)

1. Read Exercise 129 in *Spelling Wisdom, Book 3.*

2. Throughout the book, *The Reluctant Dragon,* Kenneth Grahame never gives the main character a name. Why do you suppose *Boy* is capitalized?

   _____

   _____

3. What job is the dash doing in the fifth sentence?

   _____

4. Why do you suppose the author repeated the phrase "there had been a fight" four times in this passage?

   _____

   _____

   _____

5. Alphabetize the following list of authors from previous exercises. (Look back at Lesson 40 if you need to review how to alphabetize names correctly.)

   Kenneth Grahame   _____

   Jules Verne   _____

   Carlo Collodi   _____

   William Wordsworth   _____

   Johann Wyss   _____

   Benjamin Franklin   _____

   Mark Twain   _____

6. Study the exercise until you are prepared for dictation.

Lesson 130
(from Exercise 130, Flamingoes)

1. Read Exercise 130 in *Spelling Wisdom, Book 3.*

2. Parse and analyze the following sentence from the exercise. You should find two independent clauses and one dependent clause doing the job of a noun (direct object).

   On it came, greatly diminishing its rate, and we then saw that it was composed of flamingoes.

3. Explain what a metaphor and a simile are, including the difference between the two.

   _____

   _____

4. Find the simile near the end of the exercise and describe what is being compared.

   _____

   _____

5. Find the simile near the end of Exercise 124 and describe what is being compared.

   _____

   _____

6. Think of another word that could be used in place of each verb/verbal listed below from the exercise. As always, keep context in mind. Circle which word in each pair you think is most descriptive.

sweeping	_____
alighted	_____
arranged	_____
marched	_____
arching	_____
digging	_____
perched	_____

7. Study the exercise until you are prepared for dictation.

Parse above the words:	PRO = pronoun	N = common noun	PN = proper noun	AV = action verb
	LV = linking verb	HV = helping verb	ADJ = adjective	ART = article
	ADV = adverb	PP = preposition	CON = conjunction	INT = interjection
	—inf— = infinitive	par = participle	ger = gerund	
Analyze below the words:	S = simple subject	P = simple predicate	DO = direct object	IO = indirect object
	PN = predicate nominative	PA = predicate adjective		
Identify clauses:	| independent clause |	< dependent clause >		

Lesson 131

(from Exercise 131, Benjamin Franklin and Electricity)

1. Read Exercise 131 in *Spelling Wisdom, Book 3.*

2. Parse and analyze the following sentence from the exercise. Look carefully for the direct object; it is split by a prepositional phrase.

    Franklin proposed to use in his experiment a sharp-pointed iron rod rising from the top of some

    high tower.

3. For each word or phrase below, tell what word in the exercise it modifies.
    *   wholly_____
    *   in his experiment _____
    *   immortal _____

4. Explain how each sentence's meaning changes when the modifier is moved to a different place.

    Franklin proposed to use a sharp-pointed iron rod in his experiment rising from the top of some high tower.

    _____

    This leads us to the immortal story of how he flew his kite.

    _____

5. Explain what job the colon is doing in the first paragraph.

    _____

6. Explain what job the dashes are doing in the final paragraph.

    _____

7. Study the exercise until you are prepared for dictation.

Parse above the words:	PRO = pronoun	N = common noun	PN = proper noun	AV = action verb
	LV = linking verb	HV = helping verb	ADJ = adjective	ART = article
	ADV = adverb	PP = preposition	CON = conjunction	INT = interjection
	—inf— = infinitive	par = participle	ger = gerund	
Analyze below the words:	S = simple subject	P = simple predicate	DO = direct object	IO = indirect object
	PN = predicate nominative	PA = predicate adjective		
Identify clauses:	| independent clause |	< dependent clause >		

Lesson 132
(from Exercise 132, Robert Bruce and the Spider)

1. Read Exercise 132 in *Spelling Wisdom, Book 3*.

2. Tell the story of the poem in your own words.

_____

_____

_____

_____

_____

3. Did you notice that the eighth stanza switches verb tense: from past to present? Why do you suppose the poet did that?

_____

_____

4. Define *clew*, taking into consideration the context of the first stanza.

_____

5. In the poem, find
   - a homonym for *hire* _____
   - an antonym for *hopefulness* _____
   - a synonym for *gossamery* _____

6. Analyze the poem's structure.
   - Number of stanzas: _____
   - Lines per stanza: _____
   - Rhyme scheme: _____
   - Syllables per line (most lines): _____

7. Define *iambic foot* and tell whether this poem is in iambic meter.

_____

_____

8. Study the poem until you are prepared for dictation.

Lesson 133

(from Exercise 133, Working for Father)

1. Read Exercise 133 in *Spelling Wisdom, Book 3.*

2. From the exercise, find an example of each of the following types of sentences:

   Simple _____

   _____

   Compound _____

   _____

   Complex _____

   _____

   Compound-complex _____

   _____

3. Parse and analyze the following sentence from the exercise. Pay attention to how the words of the sentence are arranged.

   With it he wanted to buy himself a new suit.

4. Parse and analyze the following sentence. which also has an interesting word order.

   Ink he had none, so he used the juice of blackberries or cherries.

5. Tell whether the conjunction that begins the second clause in that sentence is coordinating or subordinating.

   _____

6. Explain why there is a comma after "Among other things," at the beginning of the second paragraph.

   _____

7. Study the exercise until you are prepared for dictation.

Parse above the words:	PRO = pronoun	N = common noun	PN = proper noun	AV = action verb
	LV = linking verb	HV = helping verb	ADJ = adjective	ART = article
	ADV = adverb	PP = preposition	CON = conjunction	INT = interjection
	—inf— = infinitive	par = participle	ger = gerund	
Analyze below the words:	S = simple subject	P = simple predicate	DO = direct object	IO = indirect object
	PN = predicate nominative	PA = predicate adjective		
Identify clauses:	| independent clause |	< dependent clause >		

Lesson 134
(from Exercise 134, Dorothy Prepares to Travel)

1. Read Exercise 134 in *Spelling Wisdom, Book 3.*

2. Parse and analyze the following sentence from the exercise. Watch for a compound predicate verb, an infinitive, and a participle.

   Toto ran over to the trees and began to bark at the birds sitting there.

   Analyzing Tip: Use the three-step process to help you analyze a sentence. See page 154 for details.

3. Explain why the comma is used in the following sentence.

   She took a little basket and filled it with bread from the cupboard, laying a white cloth over the top.

   _____

   _____

4. Why is there no comma before *and* in that sentence?

   _____

   _____

5. Complete the chart below that details how to use *lay* and *lie*. Circle the word on the chart that is used in the participial phrase in #3 (with an *-ing* suffix).

	Present	Past	Past Participle
Lie (to _____)	_____	_____	*Lain*
Lay (to _____)	_____	_____	_____

6. Study the exercise until you are prepared for dictation.

Parse above the words:	PRO = pronoun	N = common noun	PN = proper noun	AV = action verb
	LV = linking verb	HV = helping verb	ADJ = adjective	ART = article
	ADV = adverb	PP = preposition	CON = conjunction	INT = interjection
	—inf— = infinitive	par = participle	ger = gerund	
Analyze below the words:	S = simple subject	P = simple predicate	DO = direct object	IO = indirect object
	PN = predicate nominative	PA = predicate adjective		
Identify clauses:	| independent clause |	< dependent clause >		

Lesson 135
(from Exercise 135, Straight Paths)

1. Read Exercise 135 in *Spelling Wisdom, Book 3.*

2. Parse and analyze the following sentence from the exercise.

   There was a large meadow nearby with a grand old oak tree standing in the center of it.

3. Explain why there is a comma after *Now* and after *boys* in the fourth paragraph of the exercise.

   _____

   _____

4. For each of the following phrases or clauses from the exercise, tell what kind it is and what job it is doing.

   standing in the center of it
   Kind of phrase: _____
   Job: _____

   at a given signal
   Kind of phrase: _____
   Job: _____

   that is straight at all
   Kind of clause: _____
   Job: _____

   how we all contrived to go so crooked
   Kind of clause: _____
   Job: _____

5. Explain the difference between a phrase and a clause.

   _____

   _____

6. In the fifth paragraph, you will see a possessive proper noun. What belongs to Harry Armstrong? (Hint: You won't find the answer in that sentence; it is an understood subject. Look in the preceding sentences to find the answer.)

   _____

7. Study the exercise until you are prepared for dictation.

Lesson 136

(from Exercise 136, The Gettysburg Address)

1. Read Exercise 136 in *Spelling Wisdom, Book 3*.

2. Parse and analyze the following sentence from the exercise. Go ahead. You can do it!

   Four score and seven years ago our fathers brought forth on this continent a new nation, conceived in liberty and dedicated to the proposition that all men are created equal.

3. For each phrase or clause listed below, tell what word in the exercise it modifies.

   Four score and seven years ago _____

   on this continent _____

   conceived in liberty _____

   dedicated to the proposition _____

   that all men are created equal _____

4. The Gettysburg Address is short but powerful. Do some Internet research (with adult supervision) and describe the occasion for which Abraham Lincoln wrote and delivered that speech.

   _____

   _____

5. Notice how many times he used *dedicate* or *dedicated* in that address. Summarize what idea he gave each of the six times he used those words.

   _____

   _____

   _____

   _____

   _____

6. Study the exercise until you are prepared for dictation.

Parse above the words:	PRO = pronoun	N = common noun	PN = proper noun	AV = action verb
	LV = linking verb	HV = helping verb	ADJ = adjective	ART = article
	ADV = adverb	PP = preposition	CON = conjunction	INT = interjection
	—inf— = infinitive	par = participle	ger = gerund	
Analyze below the words:	S = simple subject	P = simple predicate	DO = direct object	IO = indirect object
	PN = predicate nominative	PA = predicate adjective		
Identify clauses:	| independent clause |	< dependent clause >		

Lesson 137
(from Exercise 137, Escape)

1. Read Exercise 137 in *Spelling Wisdom, Book 3.*

2. Complete the chart below that details how to use *lay* and *lie.* Circle the word on the chart that is used in the first sentence of the exercise. Keep in mind the verb tense.

	Present	Past	Past Participle
Lie (to _____)	_____	_____	_____
Lay (to _____)	_____	_____	_____

3. For each of the following sentences from the exercise, tell what the *and* is connecting.

   He watched quietly and soon saw a large fox coming towards him. _____

   Then he sprang up quickly and seized it by the tail. _____

   It ran into a narrow cleft which he had not seen before and then through a long, dark passage which was barely large enough for a man's body. _____

   He let go of the fox, and it ran out. _____

   Here the rocks were smaller, and he soon loosened them enough to allow him to squeeze through. _____

   In a short time he was free and in the open air. _____

4. Explain the guideline for using a comma before the conjunction *and.*

   _____

   _____

5. How is the subject a key in knowing when to use a comma in those situations?

   _____

   _____

   _____

   _____

6. Study the exercise until you are prepared for dictation.

Lesson 138
(from Exercise 138, First Composition)

1. Read Exercise 138 in *Spelling Wisdom, Book 3*.

2. Parse and analyze the following sentence from the exercise.

   Just behind the schoolhouse was Mr. Finney's barn.

3. The phrase "behind the schoolhouse" modifies what word in that sentence? _____

4. Parse and analyze the following sentence from the exercise.

   Before the half hour was ended he had written a very neat composition on his slate.

5. The clause "before the half hour was ended" is doing what job in the sentence? _____

6. The phrase "on his slate" modifies which word? _____

7. Parse and analyze the following sentence from the exercise.

   He then went into the house and waited while the teacher read it.

8. The clause "while the teacher read it" is doing what job in the sentence? _____

9. Study the exercise until you are prepared for dictation.

Parse above the words:	PRO = pronoun	N = common noun	PN = proper noun	AV = action verb
	LV = linking verb	HV = helping verb	ADJ = adjective	ART = article
	ADV = adverb	PP = preposition	CON = conjunction	INT = interjection
	—inf— = infinitive	par = participle	ger = gerund	
Analyze below the words:	S = simple subject	P = simple predicate	DO = direct object	IO = indirect object
	PN = predicate nominative	PA = predicate adjective		
Identify clauses:	| independent clause |	< dependent clause >		

Lesson 139

(from Exercise 139, How the Leaves Came Down)

1. Read Exercise 139 in *Spelling Wisdom, Book 3.*

2. Narrate the poem. What is it about?

   _____

   _____

   _____

   _____

   _____

3. Describe the tone of the poem. What kind of emotions are conveyed in its word choices and sentences? Cite examples.

   _____

   _____

   _____

   _____

4. Who do you think is the "one from far away" mentioned in the sixth stanza?

   _____

5. Now analyze the poem's structure.
   - Number of stanzas: _____
   - Lines per stanza: _____
   - Rhyme scheme: _____
   - Syllables per line (most lines): _____
   - Foot (give the official name): _____
   - Foot per line (give the official name): _____

6. Study the poem until you are prepared for dictation.

Lesson 140
(from Exercise 140, 1 Corinthians 13)

1. Read Exercise 140 in *Spelling Wisdom, Book 3*.

2. Parse and analyze the following sentence from the exercise. Look carefully at word order.

   And now abideth faith, hope, and charity, these three; but the greatest of these is charity.

3. Explain each type of sentence below. Identify which type the sentence in #2 is and how you know.

   Simple _____

   _____

   Compound _____

   _____

   Complex _____

   _____

   Compound-complex _____

   _____

   The sentence in #2 _____

   _____

4. Underline the two noun clauses in the following sentence from the exercise and tell what job they are doing.

   But when that which is perfect is come, then that which is in part shall be done away.

   _____

(Lesson continues on next page)

Parse above the words:	PRO = pronoun	N = common noun	PN = proper noun	AV = action verb
	LV = linking verb	HV = helping verb	ADJ = adjective	ART = article
	ADV = adverb	PP = preposition	CON = conjunction	INT = interjection
	—inf— = infinitive	par = participle	ger = gerund	
Analyze below the words:	S = simple subject	P = simple predicate	DO = direct object	IO = indirect object
	PN = predicate nominative	PA = predicate adjective		
Identify clauses:	| independent clause |	< dependent clause >		

5. Complete the chart to explain the difference between the three types of verbals.

Verbals	Forms	Jobs
Gerund	_____	_____
Participle	_____	_____
Infinitive	_____	_____
	_____	_____

6. Identify each verbal as you find it in the following sentence from Exercise 129. Mark *par* for participle, —*inf*— for infinitive, and *ger* for gerund. (You should find one participle, one infinitive, and two gerunds.)

Banquets are always pleasant things, consisting mostly, as they do, of eating and drinking; but

the specially nice thing about a banquet is that it comes when something's over and there's

nothing more to worry about and tomorrow seems a long way off.

7. Study the exercise until you are prepared for dictation.

Comma Guidelines

Commas are often overused, underused, and misused. You have already learned some comma guidelines in previous *Using Language Well* books; those guidelines are listed below.

Other comma guidelines are directly tied to knowing how to analyze a sentence. You will be learning them as you progress through the lessons in this book. Record below the additional eight comma guidelines that you discover as you work through the lessons. They will help you use commas effectively in your writing.

Use a comma
- to separate items in a series
- to separate the day and year in a date
- at the end of the salutation of an informal letter
- to set off a direct address

-
-
-
-
-
-
-
-

Using commas in dialogue

If the dialogue tag is after the quoted material: "Quoted material," dialogue tag.

If the dialogue tag is before the quoted material: Dialogue tag, "Quoted material."

If the dialogue tag splits one sentence into parts: "Quoted," dialogue tag, "material."

If the dialogue tag is between two sentences: "Quoted material," dialogue tag. "Quoted material."

If the quoted material is a question in itself:

"Quoted material?" dialogue tag.

Dialogue tag, "Quoted material?"

"Quoted first part of," dialogue tag, "material?"

"Quoted material," dialogue tag. "More quoted material?"

Analyzing Sentences Step-by-Step

Step 1: Find the Verbs and Their Subjects

First, look for any verbs, then look for the subject that belongs to each verb. Mark those pairs as subjects and predicates, as directed in the lessons.

You will be able to narrow down the options much quicker if you note and mentally **set aside any modifiers**. Modifiers will not be a subject or a predicate verb. Be sure to disregard any part of speech that is acting as a modifier (prepositional phrases, adjectives, adverbs). You might want to strike a line through them to help you mentally set them aside.

Remember: As you are looking for verbs, you may come across a verbal, or verb form (participle, infinitive, or gerund). Determine whether that verbal is doing the job of a modifier. If it is modifying (participles and some infinitives), disregard it. If the verbal is not modifying (gerunds and some infinitives), it will be acting as a noun. Check to see whether it is the subject. If the verbal is the subject, mark it as such; if it is not, keep that verbal in mind as you move to the next step.

Step 2: Look for the Main Patterns

Second, determine whether the sentence you are analyzing has any subject complements that go with the subjects and verbs you have identified. Not all sentences will have them, but many will. You will find mainly three sentence patterns:

Sentence Pattern 1: Subject – Action Verb – Direct Object (noun)
Sentence Pattern 2: Subject – Linking Verb – Predicate Nominative (noun)
Sentence Pattern 3: Subject – Linking Verb – Predicate Adjective (adjective)

Mark any subject complements, as directed in the lessons. Also keep in mind that some sentences will have an indirect object inserted into the pattern; be sure to mark those too:

Subject – Action Verb – (*to* or *for*) Indirect Object – Direct Object

Remember: Some verbals (gerunds and some infinitives) can act as subject complements; watch for those instances.

Step 3: Determine the Clauses

Every time you see a verb paired with a subject, it will be in a clause. The final step is to identify each of the clauses and determine whether it is independent or dependent.

Every sentence must have at least one independent clause—a clause that can stand on its own without any additional information. Mark the independent clause(s) first.

Some sentences will also have one or more dependent clauses. If a clause does not give complete information by itself, but depends on another clause to complete its thought, mark that clause as a dependent clause.

Remember: If a clause starts with a subordinating conjunction, the clause is dependent. Learn the list of subordinating conjunctions on page 151 to help you.

Finally, determine what job any dependent clause is doing. It may just be a modifier; but it might be acting as the subject or a subject complement. If you have not found one of those pieces of the pattern in Step 2, check to see if any dependent clause might complete the pattern.

Analyzing a sentence can help you understand an author's overall intent or meaning. As with anything worthwhile, practice will help the process become easier and more enjoyable.

Helpful Word Lists

Prepositions
about
above
across
after
against
along
among
around
at
before
behind
beneath
beside
between
beyond
by
concerning
despite
down
during
following
for
from
in
including
into
like
near
of
off
on
onto
out
over
since
through
throughout
to
toward
under
until
up
upon
with
within
without

Conjunctions
Coordinating
and
but
for
nor
or
so
yet

Subordinating
after
although
as
as if
as long as
as much as
as soon as
as though
because
before
even
even if
even though
if
if when
if only
if then
in order that
inasmuch
just as
lest
now
now since
now that
now when
once
provided
provided that
rather than
since
so that
supposing
than
that
though
till
unless
until
when
whenever
where
where if
whereas
wherever
whether
which
while
who
whoever
why

Linking Verbs
appear
are
be
become
been
being
called
feel
grow
is
look
remain
seem
smell
stay
taste
was
were

Helping Verbs
am
are
be
been
being
can
could
did
do
does
had
has
have
is
may
might
must
shall
should
was
were
will
would